FOOTBALL'S
STUNTING DEFENSES

Charles Roche

Parker Publishing Company, Inc.   West Nyack, N.Y.

© 1982 by

Parker Publishing Company, Inc

West Nyack, New York

Library of Congress Cataloging in Publication Data

Roche, Charles
   Football's stunting defenses.

   Includes index.
   1. Football—Defense. 2. Football coaching.
I. Title
GV951.18.R63   796.332'2   82-6321
ISBN   0-13-324020-7   AACR2

Printed in the United States of America

To my wife, Betty Lou,
for her patience and understanding;
And to Billy and Jennifer
whom I love very much

CONTENTS

HOW STUNTING DEFENSES
CAN HELP YOUR PROGRAM

Most high school football programs are not blessed with an abundance of football talent or great size on a yearly basis. If this is true in your program, then this book will help improve your team's performance on defense. If you are fortunate to be the exception, then the defensive program presented in this book will help you take those good players and make them a great defensive team.

Since its introduction, the defensive program presented in this book has been instrumental in keeping our teams competitive when we had players of average size and ability. We have been successful with 165 pound defensive tackles! Regardless of the ability or size of the athletes in your coaching situation, this program will make playing defensive football more enjoyable, make your players more enthusiastic and lead to a more successful team performance on defense. It has been our experience that this defensive scheme has helped us to win games with average high school athletes and to win championships when we have had good athletes.

Football's Stunting Defenses is the result of developing and using a comprehensive stunting defensive program that has proven to be very successful regardless of the size or overall athletic ability of our players.

This complete defensive program includes stunting combinations from both even and odd fronts; zone, man to man and combination pass coverages; goal line and short yardage defenses; special stunting combinations to stop today's popular offenses; and drills that are used to teach and improve all aspects of the defensive program. In addition, this book includes a chapter on the preparation of the defensive game plan along with the daily practice schedule.

The material in *Football's Stunting Defenses* while being comprehensive is also very easy to teach. Imagine, a defensive package that is so easy to teach that your players will enjoy going on the field to "attack" the offense.

Simplicity, while very important, is not the only advantage to our program of stunting defenses. Flexibility, in terms of personnel placement and adjustments during the game, has also been a key factor in our defensive success. The success is directly related to the aggressive nature of the defense. All coaches expect their players to be aggressive and attack when on offense, but then, have their defenders react to something the opponent does when on defense. When playing the stunting defense our players are attacking the opposition on both offense and defense, which has made our overall football philosophy much more consistent.

The concepts of simplicity and flexibility are closely related. As you read this book, notice that the defensive team is divided into three groups: linemen, linebackers and safeties. The positions within each group are interchangeable. This idea of interchangeable positions is a major factor in the success of our defense. Each player must learn the assignments and techniques for his group and not for an individual position. For example, once a lineman knows the techniques and terminology that apply to our Front Four, he will be able to play any position along the defensive front.

This combination of simplicity and flexibility, which is the key to the *Football's Stunting Defenses,* allows you to move your personnel from week to week or even during the game. This will insure the best possible defensive alignment for each opponent. Specific examples of this flexibility can be found in Chapter 1.

Since changing to our present stunting defense, as presented in this book, we have averaged a defensive shutout once every three games, given up one touchdown or less in 60% of our games, and in one season allowed only 49 points in eleven games!

Football's Stunting Defenses, with more than 160 diagrams, is a comprehensive guide that is easy to teach, features interchangeable positions, is flexible enough to stop any of today's offenses, will develop an aggressive, enthusiastic attitude among your players, emphasizes quickness over size, and is very difficult for your opponent to prepare for.

The material in this book has been the key to our football program's development from a point where we hoped we could win to one where we now think we should win. It can do the same for your program!

Charles Roche

ACKNOWLEDGMENTS

This book is the result of input from a large number of sources. When the stunting defense was first introduced, it was based on Tom Simonton's book, *How to Coach Football's 44 Stack Defense*, published by Parker Publishing Company in 1972. Much of the terminology used in this book, along with some of the diagrams in the first three chapters, can be found in Coach Simonton's book. Also, the chapter that deals with defending the wishbone contains material based on an article written by Gregg Norberg which appeared in the *Athletic Journal*, September, 1978.

I would like to thank all the people who have coached with me at Whippany Park, especially Rich Keenan, Ken Mulligan and Joe Righetti, for their suggestions and input in developing this defensive package.

A special thank you to my wife, Betty Lou, for the countless hours spent in preparing the text and to Joe Krufka and the Graphics Arts department at Whippany Park High School for their help with the diagrams.

C. R.

1

TEACHING THE BASIC
DEFENSIVE ALIGNMENT
AND RESPONSIBILITIES

Philosophy of the Stunting Defense

Our defensive philosophy can be summarized in three words: "MAKE SOMETHING HAPPEN!!!" The majority of our alignments put eight people close to the ball. From these alignments anywhere from four to eight players may be attacking the offensive front on any one play. The objective is to confuse the blocking and make the big play on defense. We rely on quickness rather than size; on penetration rather than reaction.

However, it is very important that each player be thoroughly aware of his responsibilities in the basic alignment. Very rarely, if ever, will all of the defenders be involved in a stunt on any one play. Those who are not involved in the stunt must play the basic defense. Our players are taught, "unless you are told to do something (by the defensive call), play basic." Therefore, even though our success is based on stunting and attacking the offense, the importance of the basic responsibilities must be emphasized.

How to Align the Basic Defense

Diagram 1.1 shows the alignment of the basic, even defense. The linemen are eighteen (18) inches from the ball. This distance is important as it enables the front people to stunt more effectively. The linebacker aligns directly behind the down lineman, being sure that he will be able to clear the lineman when moving laterally. The linemen and linebackers work together in units numbered one through four from left to right.

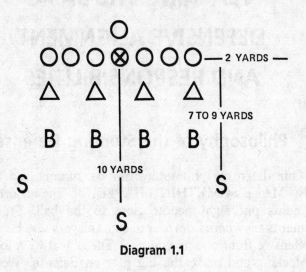

Diagram 1.1

The alignment of the safeties is shown against a balanced set. The adjustments to various formations will be discussed in Chapter 2.

Teaching the Basic Responsibilities— Linemen

When playing basic, the primary responsibility of the down lineman is to defeat the blocker directly in front of him. It is extremely important that the defensive lineman does not pick a side. The shoulders and hips must stay parallel to the line of scrimmage. Either a two hand shiver or a forearm shiver combined with a hand shiver are the most common ways of playing the blocker. Once the blocker has been neutralized, the lineman must expect the ball to be coming at him. He must be ready to make the tackle. If the ball is not coming at him, the lineman locates the ball and pursues.

Until the ball carrier crosses the line of scrimmage, the lineman will maintain an inside-out pursuit relationship. This is so that the lineman can be in position to make the tackle when the ball carrier is forced to cut back. Once the ball has crossed the line of scrimmage, the lineman must take an angle at which he can intercept the ball carrier. Because of the stunting nature of the defense, there are no assigned lanes of pursuit because the stunting takes priority and you can not have both penetration and good pursuit.

Teaching the Basic Responsibilities— Linebackers

The primary responsibility of the linebacker is to move to the ball and make the tackle. While the four linebacker positions are interchangeable, there are some differences in their basic responsibilities.

The inside linebacker's (2 and 3) first responsibility is to fill the off tackle hole. This may change from week to week, depending on tendencies or by exchanging this responsibility with the lineman of his unit. When he fills the hole, the linebacker must keep his shoulders square and parallel to the line of scrimmage. The linebacker must also defeat the blocker with his inside arm so as not to be "caved in" by the blocker. In Diagram 1.2, the linebacker delivers the blow using the inside arm.

The outside linebackers (1 and 4) are responsible for forcing any outside play to their side. The basic key for the outside linebacker is the end or the end-wingback combination. If the linebacker reads run, he will penetrate and force the play by keeping his shoulders parallel and playing off the lead block with his inside shoulder. If the linebacker cannot make the tackle, he must force the play back and to the inside so the pursuit can make the play. When working on this technique, it is critical that the linebacker does not penetrate too deeply and take himself out of the play. We have found an aiming point of approximately one yard into the backfield to be the optimum. Another point of emphasis is that the linebacker cannot wait for the play to come to him; after his penetration, he should close to the inside without turning his body. This is very similar to an anti-trap technique used by defensive linemen.

Diagram 1.2

If, after reading his key, the outside linebacker determines that the flow is moving away, he then assumes responsibility for any reverse or counter action. On a running play, the backside linebacker pursues after he is sure there is no possibility of a counter or reverse. On a rollout or a sprintout pass, the backside linebacker will rotate as described in Chapter 4.

Diagram 1.3 shows the path of the number four linebacker reading run to his side. The linebacker must use his left shoulder to defeat the blocker and jam the hole. This is important because, by using the inside shoulder, the linebacker will be able to make the tackle if the ball carrier tries to cut to the outside.

Diagram 1.4 shows the contain position of the number four linebacker as flow goes away. Once reverse and counter possibilities have been eliminated, the linebacker will either pursue or rotate into his pass coverage.

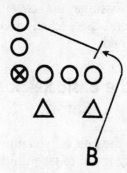

Diagram 1.3

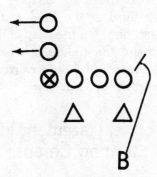

Diagram 1.4

With regard to pursuit, the inside linebackers must maintain an inside-out relationship to the ball carrier as explained in the "Fill the Hole" drill which may be found in Chapter 11. Once the ball has crossed the line of scrimmage, the inside linebackers will take an angle to cut off the ball carrier.

In all defenses, except goal line, the outside linebackers have force responsibility on the playside and contain responsibility on the backside. This contain responsibility includes reverse, outside counter, bootleg and backside screen pass. The outside linebackers are also responsible for any screen in the flat area. Whenever the outside linebacker is involved in an inside stunt, the end will assume the contain responsibility. The linebacker must remind the end any time the contain responsibility is to be switched.

Teaching the Basic Responsibilities— Safeties

The safeties are the people who must play pass first. Their primary responsibility is not to give up the "cheap" touchdown by means of a long pass. The alignment of the safeties against a balanced set is shown in Diagram 1.1. The adjustments to other formations will be discussed in Chapter 2. Each safety is responsible for one third of the field and cannot allow any receiver to get behind him. On the snap of the ball, each safety takes three steps toward the middle of his zone, while reading run or pass. Specific responsibilities involved in the basic zone coverage are discussed in Chapter 4.

Personnel Placement in the Stunting Defense

There is very little distinction made between the defensive tackles (2 and 3) and the defensive ends (1 and 4). One of the reasons for our success has been our flexibility in being able to move people in and out of the four front positions based on the needs of the team. The techniques and most of the terminology are the same for all four positions. However, once the four best defensive linemen have been chosen, we usually select the two more agile for the end positions; the other two become the tackles. Please remember that size is not the determining factor in the choice of the defensive linemen. We have been successful with defensive tackles who weigh 150-165 pounds but were aggressive and quick enough to get into the backfield.

The process of linebacker selection is similar to that of defensive lineman selection. The stronger of the linebackers will play inside and the quicker, more agile will play on the outside. We try to balance the defensive front by placing each linebacker with a lineman so that they will complement each other. For example, the inside linebacker who we feel is our best stunter would be paired with the slower of the tackles, while the slower of the inside linebackers would be paired with the quicker tackle. We also tend to have any left handed linebackers play the 3 and 4 positions so they can use their strong arm in filling the hole as described in the section on basic linebacker responsibilities.

The safeties must have the speed to be able to cover the deep zones and also be able to play man to man coverage. They should be sure tacklers, as they are the last defenders between the offense and a touchdown. Because of our rotating coverage (see Chapter 4), our most aggressive safety will play on the left side. This is because most of the teams we play show a right handed tendency. The best combination of speed, tackling ability and discipline should be the middle safety. The right safety should have the speed necessary to cover two-thirds of the field.

These are the guidelines we use in placing the personnel in the defense. However, we do not hesitate to change people around, based on scouting reports, or to substitute players in specific situations. If, for example, a team has shown a strong tendency to run to the tight end, we flip-flop our outside units so that the stronger unit is always with the tight end. Another example is to flop the left and right safeties if a team shows a strong tendency to sprint out to a certain key. Remember, flexibility is one of the major advantages to this defensive system.

2

VARYING THÈ EVEN DEFENSIVE ALIGNMENT

As indicated earlier, much of our defensive success has been due to quickness and aggressiveness. To take advantage of these attributes, we vary the alignment of the defense. In fact, we very rarely have everybody in the basic alignment. All of the variations involve the defensive personnel learning the meaning of key words combined with the direction called. Each variation will be introduced by the key word involved.

Moving the Defensive Front

The "stack" variation involves moving any number of the units in the direction called. The direction could be in (toward the center), out (away from the center), right, left, to the tight end or to the formation. The movement is from the basic alignment to an alignment in the gap in the direction called.

There may be some situations in which it is advantageous to move only the tackle or the end into a gap. This can be done by telling the tackle or the end to "stack" rather than a unit number. Diagram 2.1 shows "2 and 3 stack out," Diagram 2.2 shows "all stack left" and Diagram 2.3 shows "tackles stack out."

How to Vary the Linebacker Alignments

The key word "wide" refers only to the linebackers. The linebackers involved in the call will move over one man toward the sideline (away from the ball). If the inside linebackers are in a wide alignment, the lineman in that unit must adjust to the inside. When the wide call involves an outside linebacker to the wide side of the field, he may move over more than the one man indicated by the call. "Linebackers wide" is shown in Diagram 2.4. "2 and 3 wide" is shown in Diagram 2.5.

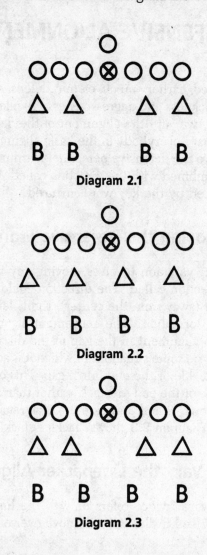

Diagram 2.1

Diagram 2.2

Diagram 2.3

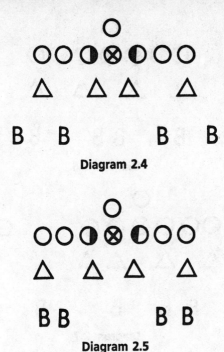

Diagram 2.4

Diagram 2.5

"Tight" also applies to the linebackers. The movement is opposite of the "wide" call. The outside linebacker aligns head up on the offensive tackle; however, the inside linebackers can only move the center-guard gaps (split six appearance). It is important that the movement of the linebackers be lateral and they do not get too close to the line of scrimmage.

When "tight" is called, the linemen must be alert as they also have to make adjustments. The 2 and 3 linemen move to the outside eye of the guards when the inside linebackers are in a "tight" alignment. If the outside linebackers are involved in the "tight" call, they exchange the contain responsibility with the end of their unit. Any time the contain is exchanged, it is up to the linebacker to remind the end. "2 and 3 tight" is shown in Diagram 2.6. Diagram 2.7 shows "tight end tight" (the adjustment to the split end will be discussed later in this chapter).

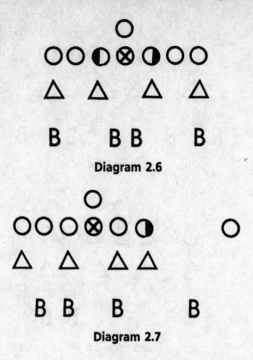

Diagram 2.6

Diagram 2.7

A final alignment variation involving the linebackers is to move any or all of them to the strength of the formation. Diagram 2.8 shows "linebackers to the formation." Again, the unit away from the formation must exchange the contain responsibility.

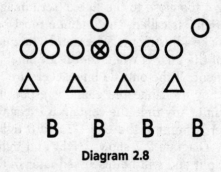

Diagram 2.8

Combining the Alignment Variations

With these alignment variations available in many combinations, it is possible to change the defensive front to meet any situation you may have to defend. The following are two examples: "1 and 4 wide, 2 and 3 stack out" (Diagram 2.9) and "front four stack in," (Diagram 2.10).

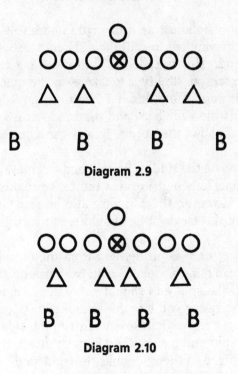

Diagram 2.9

Diagram 2.10

Formation Adjustments

To prevent the offense from gaining an advantage by moving to various formations, there are adjustments that must be made regardless of what has been called in the huddle. We have found that these adjustments become automatic without our having to spend an excess of practice time on them. The safeties and outside linebackers are responsible for the formation adjustments. In this section, the adjustments to a split end, wing back, slot (three types), and pro set will be discussed.

How to Adjust the Stunting Defense to a Split End

The normal adjustment to a split end involves the outside linebacker moving out to split the difference between the tackle and split end. This is called a "walkaway" position. The linebacker's first responsibility is to take away the quick look-in pass to the split end. After this has been accomplished, the linebacker reads the near back and the tackle as his run-pass key. Diagram 2.7 shows the normal linebacker adjustment to a split end.

The end on the side of the split end will move to the outside eye of the tackle being sure that the tackle cannot hook him to the inside. However, the end must also be able to fight through the block of the tackle if he should try to turn the end to the outside.

Because there is inside help from the outside linebacker, the safety maintains his relationship two yards outside the end as he splits. If the split end should get closer than 9 yards to the sideline, the safety will stop his lateral adjustment. The safety should not get closer than seven yards to the sideline.

If the split end is a very serious pass threat, the adjustment can be changed. When "double the split end" is called, the outside linebacker changes his alignment from the walkaway position to head up on the split end. On the snap, the linebacker holds up the split end then reads the near back and tackle. Diagram 2.11 shows "double the split end."

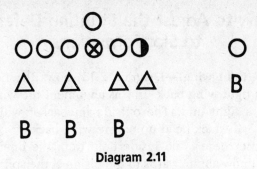

Diagram 2.11

How to Adjust the Stunting Defense to a Wing

The adjustment to a wing back is made by the outside linebacker and the safety to the side of the wing. The outside linebacker moves over, not up, until he is on the outside shoulder of the wing. He must not allow the wingback to block him down. The linebacker now reads the end-wing combination. If the wing should try to double-team the end, the linebacker will close down as shown in Diagram 1.3. Diagram 2.12 shows the normal linebacker adjustment to a wing back. The safety aligns 2 yards outside of the wing back rather than the end.

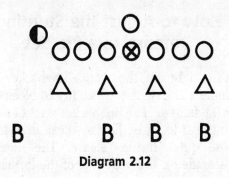

Diagram 2.12

How to Adjust the Stunting Defense
to Slot Formations

Slot—(tight wing)—Diagram 2.13 shows the normal split
end with a tight wing back. In this alignment the wing must be
treated as a tight end. The outside linebacker will not "walk
away," but will stack head up on the wing back.

Because there is no inside help from the linebacker, the
safety must now align 2 yards to the inside of the split end as the
quick inside pass is more dangerous than a pass to the outside.
The safety should always be aware of the sideline and use it to
help in his coverage.

Slot—(tight wing, tight split end)—In this alignment the
defensive end plays on the slot as a normal tight end and the
outside linebacker adjusts to the end as a wing back. This
adjustment is shown in Diagram 2.14.

Slot—(wide wing)—twins—Diagram 2.15 shows a wide slot
formation. The adjustment is similar to the normal split end
adjustment except that the linebacker splits the difference
between the wing back and the tackle rather than the split end
and tackle. The safety must be aware of the quick look-in pass to
the split end.

How to Adjust the Stunting
Defense to a Pro Set

As with the tight slot, the outside linebacker does not "walk
away" to a flanker. The tight end's ability to block on a run takes
priority over the flanker. The linebacker stacks on the tight end.
The safety to the side of the flanker must align in a position to
take away the quick inside release. The normal split end
adjustment is made on the back side of the formation. Diagram
2.16 shows the basic alignment against the pro set.

By making these adjustments with the outside units and safeties, we may still vary the alignment or stunt with any of the inside units without having the offense outflank the defense.

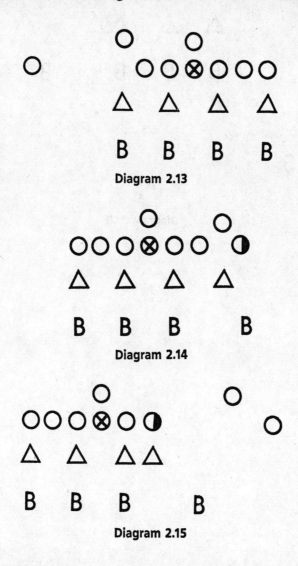

Diagram 2.13

Diagram 2.14

Diagram 2.15

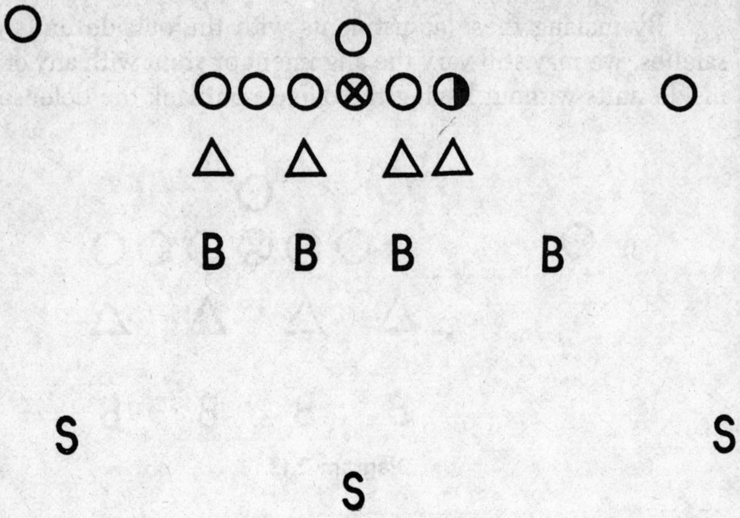

Diagram 2.16

3

STUNTING FROM THE
EVEN DEFENSE

As stated in Chapter 1, we want to "make something happen" when we are on defense. We do not want to defend our side of the line of scrimmage, but rather, we want to attack the offense. This is accomplished by stunting from the even alignment and also by stunting from the variations which will be introduced in later chapters. As with the alignment variations, each stunt is determined by a key word combined with the direction of the stunt. There are three key words in the basic defense which involve only the front lineman (gap, slant, cross). There are two key words which refer to the linebackers (fire, scrape) and there are four key words which may involve both a lineman and a linebacker (X, loop, crash, jam). The stunts will now be discussed in the order they have been introduced.

Stunting with the Defensive Linemen

Gap

This stunt involves the movement of the lineman called, on the snap, from the basic alignment through the gap in the direction called. It is important that the lineman remain parallel to the line of scrimmage as he executes the stunt. He is to get one yard into the offensive backfield and be ready to make the tackle. If the ball is moving away, he will chase the play being ready to make the tackle when the back is forced to cut back.

When "gap" is called, the linebacker behind the stunting player(s) must move in the direction opposite of the stunt to compensate for the stunt. "1 and 4 gap in" is shown in Diagram 3.1 and "2 and 3 gap to the tight end" is shown in Diagram 3.2.

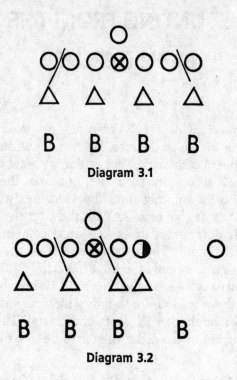

Diagram 3.1

Diagram 3.2

Slant

The "slant" stunt is similar to the "gap" stunt. However, instead of going through the gap, the lineman gets to a position on the offensive player one man over from the basic alignment. The lineman may align a little deeper from the ball when he is slanting. As with the "gap" stunt, the linebacker must compensate for the stunt. Diagram 3.3 shows "1 slant in, 3 slant out."

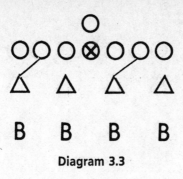

Diagram 3.3

Cross

The "cross" is the last of the stunts which involves only the front linemen. This stunt is similar to the "slant" but involves a crossing pattern. Also, the movement in the "cross" stunt is two men over as compared to a movement of one man in the "slant."

In the "cross" stunt, the number called indicates which of the linemen will move first. The other defensive linemen must know what movement is necessary to complete the crossing action. Diagram 3.4 shows "2 cross in," while "3 cross out" is shown in Diagram 3.5.

All of these stunts are executed by having the player(s) involved take an open step in the direction of the stunt. We do not want our players (on offense or defense) taking crossover steps on or near the line of scrimmage. It is our feeling that the

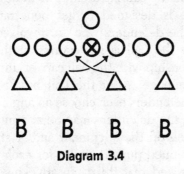

Diagram 3.4

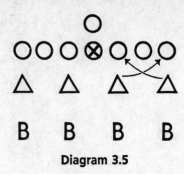

Diagram 3.5

crossover technique causes the player to lose his balance and should he be hit while in the middle of the crossover step, the defender will go down. The open step technique gives the stunting player a better base from which he can deliver a blow and take on the blocker.

In these stunts, the lineman must be careful that he does not get overextended. This means that he must keep his feet under his torso. The stunting player must always maintain a balanced football position and be ready to take on the blocker at any time. This good position also requires that, as he steps to the stunt, the lineman must keep his hips and shoulders parallel to the line of scrimmage. After the initial stunt has been completed, the lineman must be able to move in either direction should the ball not be coming at him. As indicated in Chapter 1, when a defense is designed to get penetration, it sacrifices pursuit. All of the defenders who are involved in a stunt will, after being sure the ball is not coming at them, maintain an inside-out relationship with the ball carrier until the ball crosses the line of scrimmage. After the ball has crossed the line of scrimmage the defenders each choose an angle to cut off the ball carrier. Because the defenders may be at a number of different places, depending on the alignment and/or stunt called, there are no predetermined pursuit angles for each position. It must again be emphasized that this is an attacking defense and you cannot attack and pursue at the same time.

Stunting with the Linebackers

Fire

"Fire" is the most common of the linebacker stunts. The linebacker(s) involved in the stunt penetrate through the gap of the side called. As with the linemen, the shoulders and hips must stay parallel to the line as the stunt is executed. When stunting, the linebacker must expect the ball to be coming at him. The linebacker must always be in position to make the tackle. "1 and 3 fire in" is shown in Diagram 3.6, while Diagram 3.7 shows "2 and 4 fire right."

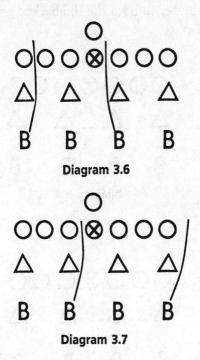

Diagram 3.6

Diagram 3.7

Scrape

The "scrape" technique is used by the 2 and 3 linebackers. Although described as a stunt, the linebacker involved does not cross the line of scrimmage. Scraping occurs as the result of reading a key—usually the guard, but sometimes the fullback. The movement involves the linebacker getting to a position one man over; being able to either fill the hole or maintain an inside-out pursuit relationship. Diagram 3.8 shows the 3 linebacker reading the guard and moving to the center. From this position he locates the ball and either makes the tackle or maintains his inside-out relationship and pursues looking for the cutback. Diagram 3.9 shows the 2 linebacker reacting to the fullback.

As with the linemen, all of the linebacker stunts begin with an open step in the direction of the call. It is very important that the defenders remain parallel to the line of scrimmage whenever possible. It is better to have the linebacker give a little ground

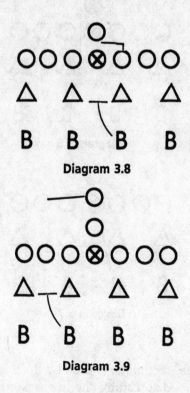

Diagram 3.8

Diagram 3.9

while remaining parallel than to have him get his body turned. The drills used to keep the linebacker parallel are described in Chapter 11.

How to Combine Stunts with the Linemen and Linebackers

X

The "X" stunt is the most common of the stunts that involve both a lineman and a linebacker. The "X" involves the lineman of the unit gapping in one direction while the linebacker "fires" in the opposite direction. The linebacker tells the lineman which direction to go. It is important that the direction of the stunting unit vary. If the linebacker always goes in the same direction, it becomes easier for the offense to block this stunt. With the "X" stunt, there can be between five and eight people attacking the offense from a single alignment. Diagram 3.10 shows "2 and 3 X."

A variation of the "X" stunt that has been very successful is called "odd or even X." This stunt involves two units Xing at the same time. The units involved are determined by the strength of the offensive formation. When the offense is strong to the left, units one and three (odd) will stunt and when the offense is

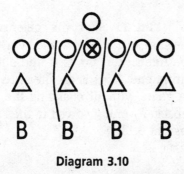

Diagram 3.10

strong to the right, units two and four (even) will stunt. Diagrams 3.11 (odd) and 3.12 (even) show the "odd or even X" possibilities.

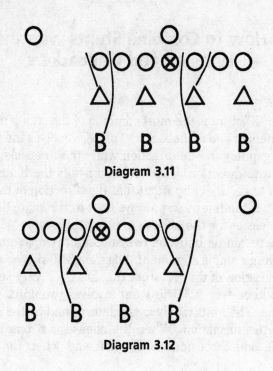

Diagram 3.11

Diagram 3.12

Loop

The "loop" stunt involves the defensive end and the linebacker of the unit inside of the end. On the snap, the end slants in and the linebacker moves to the outside, penetrating behind the slanting end. This is an alternate way to attack the outside running game without changing the pass coverage, as the outside linebacker is not involved in the stunt. "Loop right" is shown in Diagram 3.13.

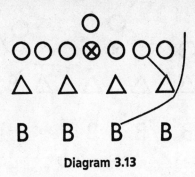

Diagram 3.13

Crash

The "crash" stunt has been very successful against the option. The stunt involves the outside unit(s) and is usually called to the right or left. However, the crash stunt may be executed to the tight end, the formation or any other direction that will give the defense an advantage. After the offense has set, the outside linebacker moves up to the line of scrimmage. On the snap, the linebacker closes down the off tackle hole on the offensive side of the line of scrimmage. If there is a wing back, the linebacker must move in front of the wing on the stunt. The end holds up the offensive end and contains to the outside. Diagram 3.14 shows "crash left" while Diagram 3.15 shows "crash to the wing."

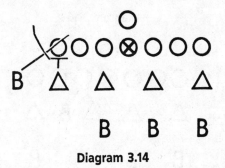

Diagram 3.14

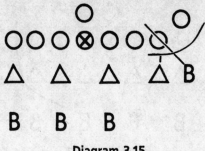

Diagram 3.15

Jam

This stunt can be used to neutralize a blocker who has been exceptionally effective. When jamming the center or the tackles, only the linemen are involved. The stunt is executed by having the lineman on either side of the blocker slant to his head.

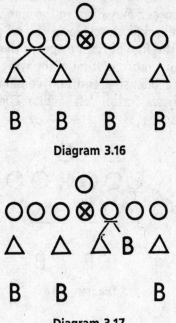

Diagram 3.16

Diagram 3.17

Diagram 3.16 shows "jam the left tackle." To "jam" a guard or an end, the unit aligned on that player must execute the stunt. The lineman moves to the inside shoulder and the linebacker comes up to the line of scrimmage on the outside shoulder. On the snap, the defensive unit drives the blocker into the backfield. "Jam the right guard" is shown in Diagram 3.17.

Using the Stunts in Combination to Attack the Offense

Once the key words have been mastered, these stunts may be used in combination. This combination of alignment variations, stunts and sound planning results in a basic defense that is able to easily adjust to, and attack, the strength of any offense.

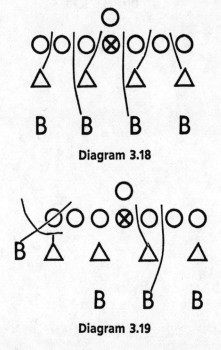

Diagram 3.18

Diagram 3.19

"2 and 3 X, 1 and 4 gap in" (Diagram 3.18), "crash left, 3 X" (Diagram 3.19) and "2 and 3 tight, 1 and 4 fire in" (Diagram 3.20) are only a few examples of the vast number of combinations possible in the basic defense. Combinations that have been successful against specific offensive strengths are discussed in Chapter 7.

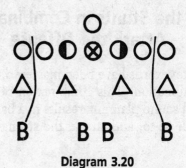

Diagram 3.20

4

ZONE PASS COVERAGE
IN THE STUNTING DEFENSE

The basic pass coverage is a zone coverage. The first year this defense was used, we played four short and three deep zones in all situations. Upon evaluation of that season, it was found that the straight zone coverage did not defend the corner to our satisfaction. Since that time, our basic pass defense has been a rotating zone coverage.

Rushing the Passer—The Front Four

The main responsibility for rushing the passer belongs to the linemen. The rush should be from the outside-in to prevent the quarterback from breaking out of the pocket. Diagram 4.1 shows the basic pass rush of the linemen.

As they rush the passer, the linemen should be alert for the draw play. It is very important that the linemen not rush deeper than the ball. The linemen cannot go past any back unless they

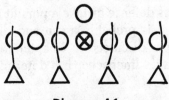

Diagram 4.1

are sure that the back does not have the football. If there is any
doubt, the potential ball carrier should be tackled.

The linemen do not have any screen responsibility. This
area of the pass coverage is assigned to the linebackers. If the
lineman "feels" a screen, he should continue his attempt to get to
the quarterback. We have had a number of quarterback "sacks"
on attempted screen passes because the linemen continued to
rush the passer, and the linebackers had the receiver covered.

Zone Pass Coverage—The Linebackers

The linebackers are normally responsible for the four short
zones. These zones are approximately thirteen yards wide and
ten yards deep. However, if one or more linebackers are involved
in a stunt, they must complete the stunt and get to the passer.
Stunting takes priority over coverage! The defensive game plan
will determine whether we pressure the quarterback or cover
the short passing zones. This decision has to be made each week
based on the information we have about the opponent. Due to
the rotation, the pass coverage is different for the outside (1 and
4) and the inside (2 and 3) linebackers.

Outside Linebackers—The outside linebacker must determine if the play is a pass or a run. To do this, he keys the
offensive end or the end-wing combination to his side. If there is
a split end and no slot, he keys the near back through the tackle
as discussed in Chapter 2. If the key releases downfield, it is
probably a pass or a run to the other side of the formation. The
linebacker should then move to his basic zone, which is the short
outside ¼ of the field (the flat). From this position, the linebacker can play pass defense or take a pursuit angle on the run.
If the key blocks, it is probably a run and the linebacker will
come up and force as discussed in Chapter 1.

Once the outside linebacker has determined the play is a

pass, he must locate the ball. If the ball is coming to him, he comes up to the outside and forces the sprintout or rollout. The outside linebacker must contain the quarterback on these plays. If the ball is moving away, the outside linebacker, after checking for reverse or counter, drops 15 yards straight down the field. Once the ball crosses the line of scrimmage, the linebacker takes a pursuit angle.

If, after locating the ball, the quarterback is dropping straight back, the linebacker stays in his basic zone.

Inside Linebackers—When playing the basic pass coverage, the inside linebackers read their key to determine if the play is a pass or a run. This key may vary from week to week. As with the outside linebacker, once the play is determined to be a pass, the inside linebacker must find the ball. On a sprintout or rollout to his side, the inside linebacker pressures the quarterback from the inside out. If the inside linebacker reads a sprintout or rollout away from him, he moves to cover the hook or curl zone on the side of the play. However, if either of the inside linebackers is stunting, the other must play the pass coverage.

On a drop back pass, the inside linebackers are responsible for the short middle zones. Again, if one is stunting, the other will play the middle of the field.

How to Stop the Screen Pass

The screen pass is the responsibility of the linebackers. On a drop back pass, as the outside linebacker moves to his zone, he must check for a back on any pattern to his side. If the back is setting up for a screen, the linebacker has to get behind the screen and make the play before the screen can get set. Any time the outside linebacker is involved in a stunt, he must remind the end, as the end now has the screen responsibility.

When the flow of the play is away from the linebacker, he must check for the backside screen before getting into the rotation.

Middle screens are the responsibility of the inside linebackers. On reading pass, as they begin to drop, they will check for the draw, then the middle screen. If they read screen, they must get behind the screen and make the play before the screen can be formed.

Role of the Safeties in the Zone Pass Defense

As with the linebackers, the outside safeties and middle safety have different basic pass coverage responsibilities. This is, again, due to the rotation used in the basic coverage.

Outside safeties—The basic alignment of the outside safeties is shown in Diagram 1.1. On the snap of the ball, they take three (3) shuffle steps toward the middle of their zones (the deep, outside ⅓ of the field). While taking these steps, the safeties read the end or the end-wing combination. By reading the key and locating the position of the ball, the safeties can determine the type of play being run. When the end blocks, the ball is probably coming to that side. If, after the third step, the ball is moving to the tackle, the safety rotates up to the flat. When rotating, it is very important that the safety maintain an outside-in relationship to the ball. The safety must not let the ball get outside of him.

This rotation of the safety gives outside-in support on the sweep as well as short, outside zone pass protection against the sprintout pass.

If, after the third step, the ball is moving to the tackle away from the safety, he rotates back and covers the deep, backside two-thirds (⅔) of the field. In all other basic situations (the ball between the tackles) the outside safeties are responsible for the deep one-third (⅓) on their side of the field.

Middle Safety—The basic alignment of the middle safety is shown in Diagram 1.1. However, as the offense starts to split receivers out, the middle safety must change his alignment. To adjust to wide receivers, the middle safety may deepen his alignment and also should cheat over to the wide side of the field. The wide side of the field, along with the formation, will determine the final alignment of the middle safety. The middle safety must be aligned so as to be able to cover the deep, outside one-third (⅓) of the field in either direction.

On the snap, the middle safety will take three (3) shuffle steps toward the middle of his zone (the deep middle ⅓ of the field). While taking the shuffle steps, the safety will determine whether the play is a run or a pass. After the three steps, the position of the ball must be located. If the ball is moving toward either tackle, the middle safety rotates to the deep, outside one-third (⅓) on the side of the flow. The safety rotates whether it is a run or a pass. This rotation of the middle safety gives the defense deep, outside coverage on the sprintout and good pursuit on the outside run.

When the ball remains between the tackles, the middle safety comes up and supports on the run, and plays the deep, middle one-third (⅓) of the field on a pass. It is very important that the middle safety not come up too quickly when he reads a run. Our safeties are taught not to support on the inside run until the ball has crossed the line of scrimmage. We feel it is better to give up a few yards on the run rather than be beat deep on the play action pass.

Diagram 4.2 shows the basic pass coverage against a drop back pass, while Diagram 4.3 shows the basic coverage against a sprintout, rollout or outside run. This coverage has proven to be more effective against the outside attack than the non-rotating zone which was used the first year this defense was played. The safeties rotate any time the ball is moving to the tackle, either run or pass.

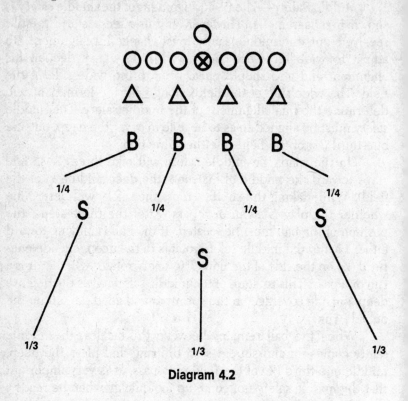

Diagram 4.2

How to Stop the Desperation Pass

During the course of a game, there may be some situations in which it would be advantageous not to rotate the defense regardless of what play is being run. This may be toward the end of the second or fourth quarter or possibly a third down with very long yardage when a long pass attempt is expected. One way to switch the defense to a non-rotating zone is by means of a call in the huddle. This call may be any term the coaches choose to indicate no rotation. We use a color call, in the huddle, to

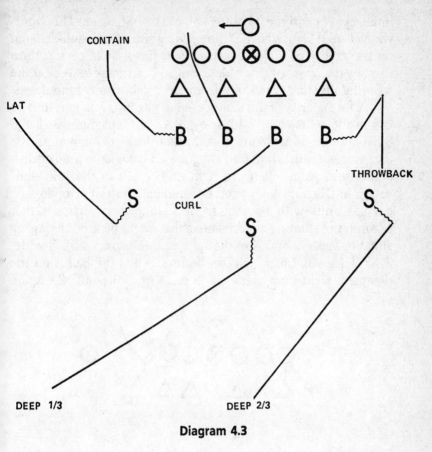

Diagram 4.3

indicate no rotation and no call for the basic coverage. In other words, if no coverage call is made in the huddle, the basic, rotating zone is played. The non-rotated zone is shown in Diagram 4.2.

How to Stunt While Playing the Zone Pass Coverage

We stunt on almost every play. If the stunt called involves one or more of the linebackers, and the play is a pass, the linebackers continue to stunt and rush the passer. The stunts which would be used in definite passing situations would depend on the ability of the quarterback and the type of pass pattern used by the offense. This is determined from week to week at the scouting meeting when the defensive game plan is formulated.

The majority of the stunts used in passing situations involve the inside units, but "odd or even X" (see Diagrams 3.11 and 3.12) may be used against a team that does not throw into the flat, or the "crash" stunt (see Diagram 3.14) could be used against a sprintout team. "Jam the tight end, crash to the split end" shown in Diagram 4.4 is another combination stunt involving the outside units with no real sacrifice in pass coverage. Other examples of stunting combinations that might be used in passing situations are: "2 or 3 X to the split end" (Diagram 4.5), "1 wide, 3 X" (Diagram 4.6) which can be used when the ball is on the defensive right hash mark, or "2 cross in, 2 fire out" (Diagram 4.7).

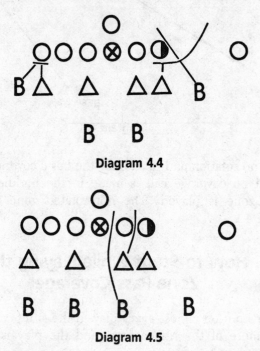

Diagram 4.4

Diagram 4.5

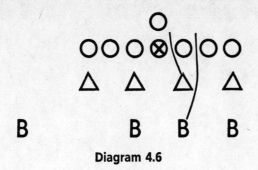

Diagram 4.6

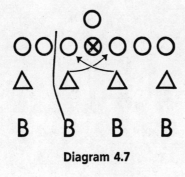

Diagram 4.7

5

STUNTING FROM THE
ODD ALIGNMENT

The preceding chapters make up what is considered to be our basic defense. However, we have found that there are some times when it is advantageous to present an odd front. For example, depending on the tendencies of the offense, it might be wise to cover the tackles or to "monster" either the formation or the wide side of the field. The defense might be able to gain an advantage by having a quick defender play against a slower center. Also, by having both an odd and even front, the opposition must spend more time in the preparation of their blocking patterns for the game. With the odd alignment as a supplement to the stunting, four man front, our defensive scheme has the flexibility to match up against any type of formation, tendency or personnel.

How to Move from the Even to the
Odd Alignment

The movement from the even to the odd defense is predetermined in the huddle. The change involves the linemen moving over one man in the direction called. The end to the side of the call does not move. The outside linebacker away from the call moves up and aligns on the end. The outside linebacker to the side called takes a "wide" alignment while the inside linebackers remain head up on the offensive guards. The result is an odd alignment that we call an overshift. Diagram 5.1 shows an overshift right, while Diagram 5.2 shows an overshift left. The overshift ("over") is usually called to the strength of the formation or to the tight end. "Over to the formation" against a pro set is shown in Diagram 5.3. Diagram 5.4 shows "over to the tight end" against a wide slot.

When the overshift has been called, the defensive front aligns in the basic 44 alignment. The defense moves to the overshift after the interior offensive linemen are set. If the opposition sets as soon as they break the huddle, the movement occurs as soon as the defense determines the direction of the overshift (formation, tight end, etc.). The offense must be set for one second before they can put the ball in play. Our experience has been that this is a sufficient amount of time to move the defensive front.

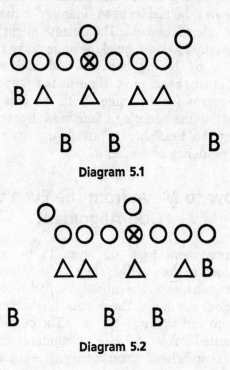

Diagram 5.1

Diagram 5.2

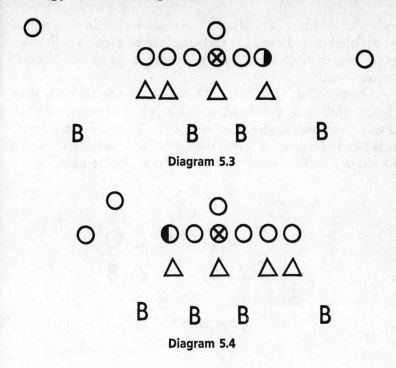

Diagram 5.3

Diagram 5.4

How to Vary the Odd Alignment

Once familiar with the overshift alignment, the defense may be introduced to alignment variations in the odd alignment similar to the variations used in the basic defense. These variations require more time to learn than those in the basic defense; the player must first move from his basic position to the overshift, then to the overshift variation. Once the players learn these variations, they will be another valuable weapon to use in attacking the offense.

There are four key words used to describe the overshift variations. The words indicate the desired change and are used with a direction to indicate the final alignment. The direction may be front (to the overshift), back (away from the overshift), right, left or any other indicator the coach may wish to use. The word "double" indicates the variation is to be used on both sides of the center. Each variation will be introduced by its appropriate key word.

Nose—The "nose" call indicates that the tackle who, after the overshift, is on the center will change his alignment with the inside linebacker in the direction called. "Over left, nose front" is shown in Diagram 5.5 and "over right, nose back" is shown in Diagram 5.6. The "nose" call *cannot* be a "double nose."

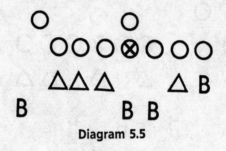

Diagram 5.5

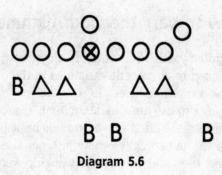

Diagram 5.6

Eagle—The "eagle" call involves the lineman who, after the overshift, is aligned on the tackle to the side of the call. The variation involves a switch in alignment between the lineman and the inside linebacker to the side of the call. Diagram 5.7

shows "over to the tight end, eagle front." "Over right, double eagle" is shown in Diagram 5.8.

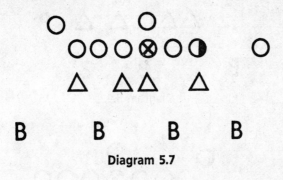

Diagram 5.7

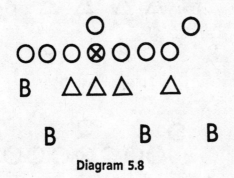

Diagram 5.8

Stack—The "stack" also involves the lineman who, after the overshift, is aligned on the tackle and the inside linebacker to the side called. The lineman moves to the guard-tackle gap, and the inside linebacker stacks behind the lineman in the gap. "Over left, stack back" is shown in Diagram 5.9. Diagram 5.10 shows "over left, double stack."

As with the basic alignment variations, it is possible to combine the variations of the overshift alignment. One example is "over left, nose front, eagle back" as shown in Diagram 5.11.

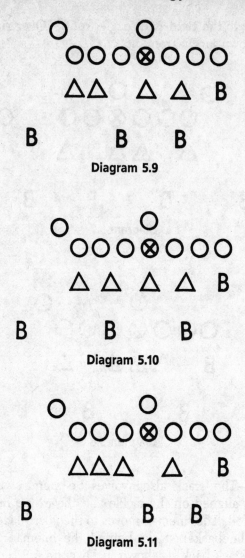

Diagram 5.9

Diagram 5.10

Diagram 5.11

Under— "Under" is an abbreviation of undershift. This term is used to move three of the four defensive linemen in a manner similar to the overshift. However, when "under" is called, the movement is one gap to the direction called, as compared to one man when "over" is called. The linebackers will be in the same alignment as in the overshift. "Under right" is shown in Diagram 5.12. The "under" can be used in the same directions as the overshift.

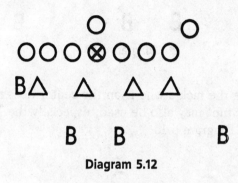

Diagram 5.12

Using Stunts to Attack the Offense from the Odd Alignment

There are a number of basic stunts that can be used from the overshift alignment. Many variations of the "gap" stunt may be called. For example "over left, nose gap front" is shown in Diagram 5.13 while Diagram 5.14 shows "over right, all gap in."

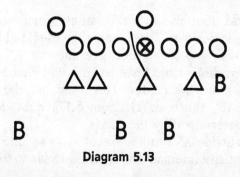

Diagram 5.13

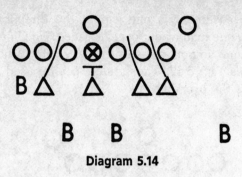

Diagram 5.14

Please notice the tackle who is on the center does not "gap in." The "crash" stunt may also be used, especially the "crash front" as shown in Diagram 5.15.

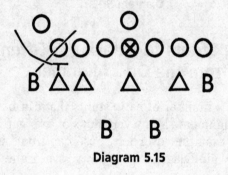

Diagram 5.15

The odd front also allows for stunts which cannot be used with the basic defense. These stunts are executed by the inside linebacker with one of the defensive linemen.

The "inside X" stunt involves an inside linebacker with the tackle who is on the center. This stunt may be to the front (Diagram 5.16), the back (Diagram 5.17), right, left or to any other key determined by the coach.

The "outside X" stunt is executed by an inside linebacker and the defensive lineman who is on the tackle to the side called.

The direction of the call may be any of those mentioned in the "inside X" description. "Over, outside X to the tight end" is shown in Diagram 5.18.

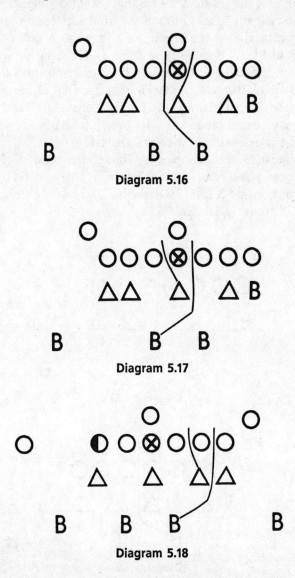

Diagram 5.16

Diagram 5.17

Diagram 5.18

In the "X" stunts from the odd alignment, the linebacker will always move to the direction called while the lineman will "gap" to the direction opposite of the call. As shown in Diagrams 5.16 and 5.17, the inside X means that the inside linebacker away from the call will attack through the front side center-guard gap while the tackle on the center will "gap" away from the call. When "outside X" is called, the lineman on the tackle will "gap" away from the call and the inside linebacker on the side of the call will attack through the tackle-end gap (see Diagram 5.18).

These "X" stunts, along with the "gap," "fire" and "crash" stunts may be combined with the overshift alignment variations to make a package that serves as an excellent complement to the basic defense. Some examples are "under, front fire in" (Diagram 5.19), "over stack front, inside X front" (Diagram 5.20), "over, crash front, inside X front" (Diagram 5.21) and "over, eagle back, outside X front" (Diagram 5.22).

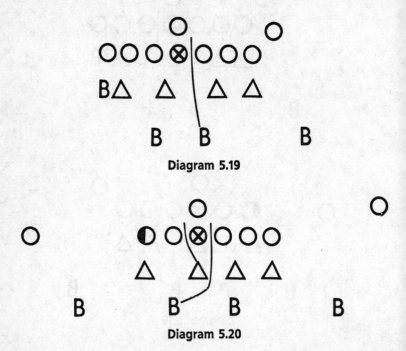

Diagram 5.19

Diagram 5.20

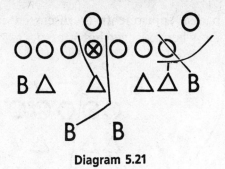

Diagram 5.21

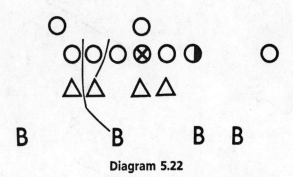

Diagram 5.22

Zone Pass Defense from the Odd Alignment

The movement from the basic defense to the overshift does not involve any change in the secondary alignment or responsibilities. The alignment change of the outside linebackers does *not* change their pass coverage. All of the overshift variations and most of the stunts are executed by the linemen with the inside linebackers. This means the basic pass coverage, as discussed in Chapter 4, can be used for all overshift calls. The sprintout to the overshift (Diagram 5.23) or away from the overshift (Diagram 5.24) can be defended with no change in coverage responsibilities. This allows for stunts involving the inside linebackers without sacrificing coverage on the perimeter of the defense.

The formation adjustments as discussed in Chapter 2 remain the same when the overshift is used.

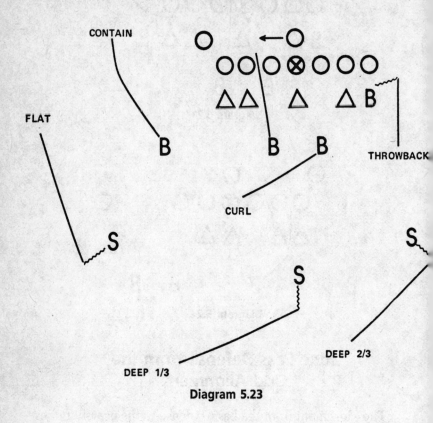

Diagram 5.23

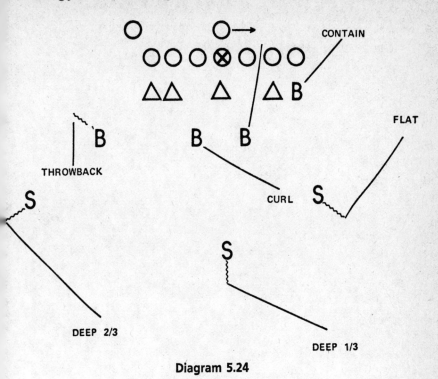

Diagram 5.24

6

ALTERNATE PASS COVERAGES
IN THE STUNTING DEFENSE

How to Move to the Four Deep Coverage

For a number of years after the introduction of the basic defense, we used the three deep alignment for man to man coverage as well as the basic zone pass coverage. During that time, we became aware of a number of drawbacks inherent in playing man to man with four linebackers and three safeties. If, for example, we assigned the safeties to cover the ends and wing back, there was no support from the secondary against the inside run. Diagram 6.1 shows how a spread alignment could move the safeties so they would be unable to help on a running play. To

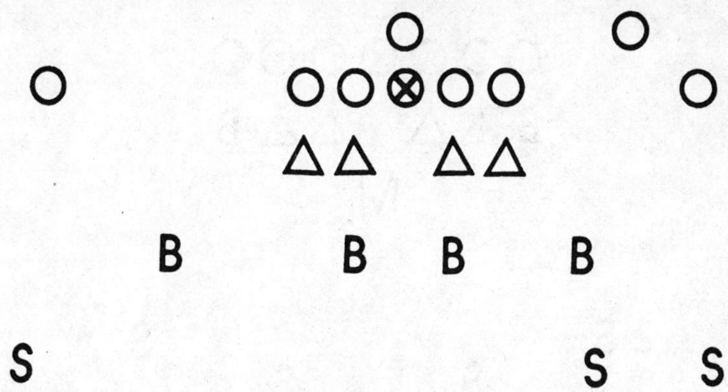

Diagram 6.1

solve the problem by using a linebacker on either an end or the wing back, presents the strong possibility of a mismatch in the coverage.

We found a solution by watching pro football on television. If the pros can bring in an extra defensive back in passing situations, why couldn't we bring in an extra safety when we wanted to play man to man coverage? After watching the game a while longer, the answer became clear: bring in a fourth safety and change the basic defense into a pro 4-3 alignment when man to man coverage is desired. This change involves moving the defensive ends to head up on the tackles, moving the outside linebackers up to play the tight ends, and substituting a fourth safety for one of the inside linebackers. All formation adjustments will, again, remain the same as in Chapter 2. The resulting 4-3 alignment is shown in Diagram 6.2.

The addition of a fourth safety allows man to man coverage on the ends and wing back while giving us a free safety to support on the run or help out the pass coverage by reading the quarterback and playing "centerfield" on a pass. Diagram 6.3 shows how the 4-3 alignment solves the problem presented by Diagram 6.1.

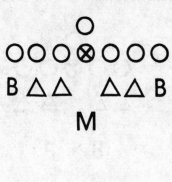

Diagram 6.2

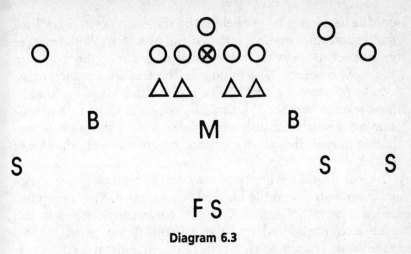

Diagram 6.3

How to Play Man to Man Using the Four Deep Coverage

Our concept of man to man coverage is slightly different from most. When playing the 4-3, we cover both ends and the wing back man for man. It should be noted that we only use the man coverage against teams who keep their backs in for pass protection or use flare patterns with the backs. Each week the safeties are assigned the position they will play. In other words, we try to match our best defender against the opponent's favorite receiver. One week the best defender might be assigned to the split end and the following week he could be covering the wing back. This method of matching the defender to the receiver takes away any advantage the offense would gain by changing formations as the defender will go with his assigned man wherever he lines up. This flexibility, along with a free safety, has been very successful against teams with one or maybe two receivers who might be considered as "big play" makers.

The underneath coverage in the 4-3 remains essentially the same as the basic coverage. The exception is, there are only three linebackers as compared to four in the basic coverage. The

outside linebackers, after holding up the end, check for any back
flaring and then cover the flat. If the play is a rollout or other
type of outside play, the outside linebacker forces, the same as in
the basic coverage. The middle linebacker, after reading pass,
checks for draw or screen. On a drop back pass, the middle
linebacker covers the short middle zone and looks for any back
coming through the line; against a sprint-out the middle linebacker mirrors the quarterback and covers the flat to the side of
the play.

The play of the linebackers against a dropback pass is shown
in Diagram 6.4, and the linebacker coverage against the sprintout is shown in Diagram 6.5. The coverage described in this
section is considered to be our "basic" coverage in the 4-3
alignment. Whenever 4-3 is called in the huddle, this coverage is
used, unless a specific call is made to indicate an alternate pass
coverage.

Using the Four Deep Zone Coverage

By making a call in the huddle, the 4-3 coverage may be
changed to a four deep zone coverage. The alignment and

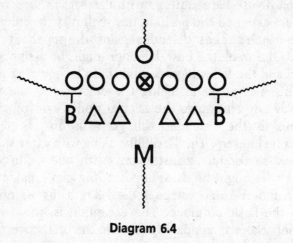

Diagram 6.4

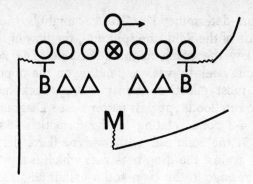

Diagram 6.5

responsibilities of the linemen and linebackers are the same as in the basic 4-3 alignment. The safeties align themselves across the field at a depth of seven yards. The outside safeties make all normal adjustments to the offensive formation. The 4-3 zone against a pro set is shown in Diagram 6.6.

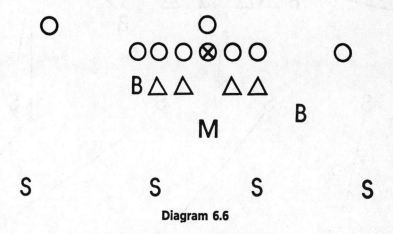

Diagram 6.6

The rotation of the 4-3 zone is very similar to the rotation used in the Oklahoma 5-2 defense. On the snap, the safeties rotate to a pre-determined key. This key might be the formation, the wide side of the field, the split end, the flow of the backs or any other key the coach might determine. The key may be changed from week to week depending on the opponent. This defense is most effective against a drop back team with a tendency to run flood type pass patterns; see Diagram 6.7 which shows the 4-3 zone rotating to the formation. As shown in Diagram 6.7, the zone call will cover the flare, flat, and three deep zones against the drop back pass which is a problem with the basic coverage in the even and overshift alignments.

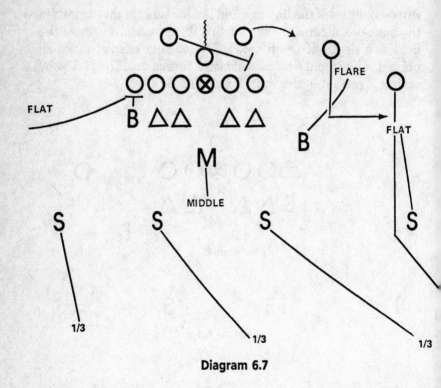

Diagram 6.7

How to Stunt While Playing a "Prevent" Defense

The prevent defense, which is not used often, is based on the 4-3 alignment and is shown in Diagram 6.8. When "prevent" is called, all coverage is zone and there is *no* rotation. The linebackers are responsible for the three short zones along with the draw play or screen pass. The three safeties, who were playing man to man, will play a normal 3 deep zone. The free safety will align ten yards behind the middle safety and play the ball, being certain that no one gets behind him.

It is important to note that we stunt when playing the "prevent" defense. Many of the lineman and linebacker stunts can be used in this alignment without any sacrifice in the deep

Diagram 6.8

coverage. Some examples include the "gap," "fire," "cross" and "crash" stunts discussed in Chapter 3. We also have some stunts that are exclusively used in the 4-3 alignment, which will be discussed later in this chapter.

How to Play Combination Coverage from the Four Deep Alignment

The 4-3 alignment also allows for combination zone and man to man coverage. This can be accomplished by having the outside linebacker cover the tight end man for man and by having the safety who would normally cover the tight end become a second free safety giving a two deep zone, five under man to man coverage.

The middle linebacker, on a pass, moves to the tight end's side and covers the first back releasing to that side. The backside outside linebacker covers the first back to that side. The combination coverage, in Diagram 6.9, is called in the huddle and allows for deep zone protection as well as most of the stunts that will be discussed in the next section.

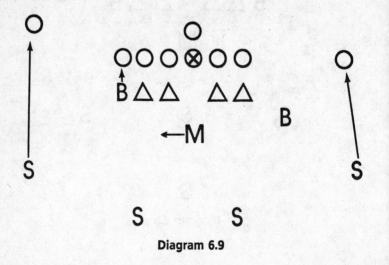

Diagram 6.9

Using Stunts to Attack the Offense While Playing Four Deep Coverage

In keeping with our philosophy of attacking the offense, a number of stunts can be used with the 4-3 alignment. There are four stunts which are commonly used. There are also some combination stunts.

Middle fire—This stunt involves the middle linebacker "firing" to the direction called. Everyone else plays his normal 4-3 responsibilities. "Middle fire to the split end" is shown in Diagram 6.10.

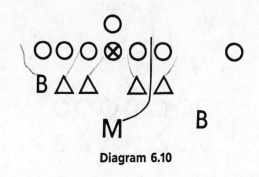

Diagram 6.10

Cross—The "cross" technique is the same as shown in Diagram 3.4. However, the "cross" stunt is limited to either of the tackles (2 or 3) crossing in. The "cross in, middle fire out" (Diagram 6.11) has been a successful combination stunt from the 4-3 alignment. A number is used with the call to indicate which lineman goes first and the direction the middle linebacker will fire. "3 cross in, middle fire at 3" is shown in Diagram 6.11.

Twist—The "twist" stunt is similar to the "cross," except the linemen are next to each other rather than one man apart. The number called indicates which lineman will go first. The first movement is in the direction called. The tackles (2 or 3) may "twist" out (Diagram 6.12) and the ends (1 or 4) may "twist" in

(Diagram 6.13). The "twist" stunt may also be combined with the "middle fire" as in "3 twist out, middle fire in at 3" (Diagram 6.14).

Diagram 6.11

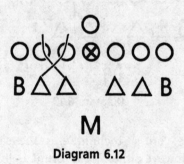

Diagram 6.12

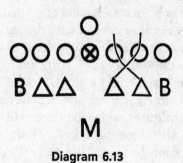

Diagram 6.13

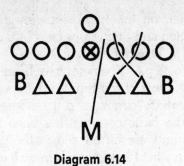

Diagram 6.14

Blitz—The "blitz" is usually executed to the split end side of the offense and is most effective against a drop back passer. The "blitz" is an overload with four defenders rushing against a maximum of three blockers.

On a "blitz" call the defensive tackle takes a definite inside pass rush while the end takes a definite outside rush. The free safety who has cheated toward the line of scrimmage attacks through the guard-tackle gap. To complete the overload, the outside linebacker also "fires" and rushes the quarterback. The

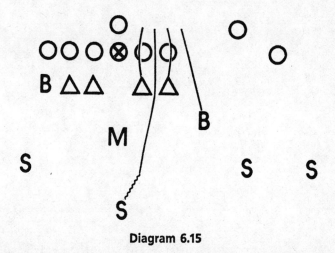

Diagram 6.15

middle linebacker, on the snap, steps toward the center, occupies his attention and then drops back into coverage. The 4-3 "blitz" is shown in Diagram 6.15.

These alternate pass coverages have been successful against teams that throw most of the time to their wide receivers. We have found that these coverages can be taught without much difficulty after the basic coverage has been learned. The 4-3 coverages and stunts are introduced in the pre-season, so the players may learn what the key words in each call mean. The 4-3 is then used in practice during the weeks we plan to use the coverages in the game. The decision as to the pass coverages we will use for a specific game is made at our weekly scouting meeting.

7

STUNTING COMBINATIONS TO STOP
ANY OFFENSIVE ATTACK

The material in the preceding chapters can be mixed and matched to form defensive stunting combinations that are only limited by the imagination and resourcefulness of the coaching staff. This chapter will show some of the combinations which have been successful in stopping various offensive attacks.

In preparing to stop any offense, we rely very heavily on the opposing team's tendencies. We plan our defense so as to stunt where we expect the opposition to attack us. We rarely, if ever, key on an individual back. Please remember that the stunting combinations shown here are not the only ones that might be used in each situation. Also, due to the special nature of the wishbone offense, it will be discussed in the next chapter.

How to Stop the Inside Running Game

Most of the stunts and variations used against the inside running game involve the number 2 and 3 units. The primary objective in stopping this type of attack is quick penetration either by aligning a defender in a gap, preferably after the offensive line has set, or by bringing a linebacker to the expected point of attack.

Some examples are "2, 3 wide—2,3 stack in" (Diagram 7.1), "front four stack in" (Diagram 7.2) or "all gap in" (Diagram 7.3). If the offense shows a tendency to run inside to a particular key, such as the tight end, then combinations such as "under, front fire in" (Diagram 7.4) or "over, inside X front" (Diagram 7.5) might be used.

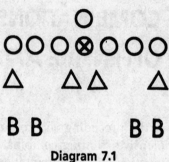

Diagram 7.1

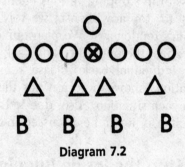

Diagram 7.2

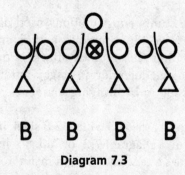

Diagram 7.3

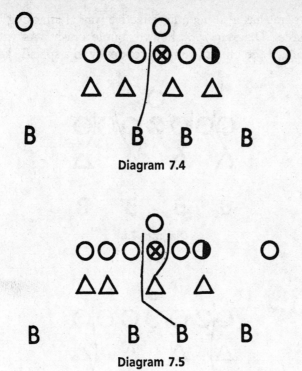

Diagram 7.4

Diagram 7.5

How to Stop the Off Tackle Play

The even alignment gives the defense a great deal of variation in stopping the off tackle play. Depending on personnel and what other areas have to be protected, any one or more of the four defenders on that side of the ball may be brought into the off tackle area. If the opponent runs the off tackle trap or power play as a basic part of its attack, it is important that the defense have a number of calls available to attack this area, disrupt the blocking pattern and free a defender to make the play.

The possibilities are as simple as "1 and 4 gap in, 2 and 3 gap out" (Diagram 7.6) or "1 and 4 fire in" (Diagram 7.7). The "crash" stunt has also been an effective way of attacking the off tackle hole. Diagram 7.8 shows "double crash." As with the inside run, if the offense shows a tendency to a specific key, the

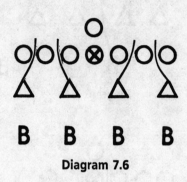

Diagram 7.6

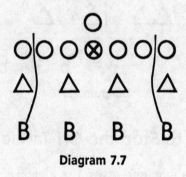

Diagram 7.7

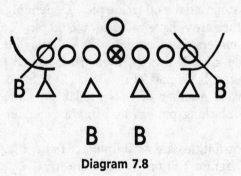

Diagram 7.8

overshift may be used. Some overshift combinations might be, "over, stack front, inside X front" (Diagram 7.9) or "over, outside X front" (Diagram 7.10).

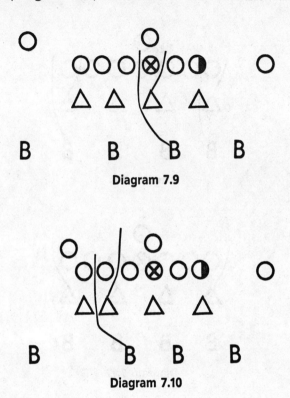

Diagram 7.9

Diagram 7.10

How to Attack the Offense at the Corner

The alignment and play of the outside linebacker in the stunting defense is instrumental in not allowing the offense to successfully attack the corner. By reading his key, when he is not stunting, the outside linebacker will be in position (as shown in Diagram 1.3) to force the power sweep or to cut off the quarterback on the rollout or sprintout. Also, the rotation as discussed in Chapter 4 will give outside support on the run should the ball cross the line of scrimmage.

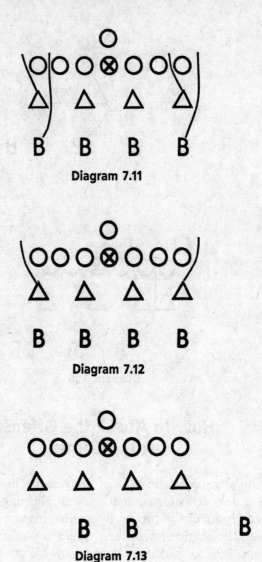

Diagram 7.11

Diagram 7.12

Diagram 7.13

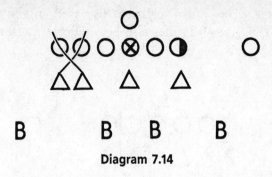

Diagram 7.14

There are a number of simple calls that have been effective in confusing blocking patterns and attacking either the outside sweep or the sprintout pass offense. Some of the combinations we have used include, "1 and 4 X" (Diagram 7.11), "1 and 4 gap out" (Diagram 7.12), "1 and 4 wide" (Diagram 7.13), "over, twist in" (Diagram 7.14) and the "crash" stunt as shown in Diagram 7.8.

How to Stop the Pro-Type Offense

The pro offense presents some problems in that there are wide receivers to both sides of the formation which may stretch the perimeter of the defense; there is also a strong side for the running attack. Against this offense it is very important to determine whether stopping the run or the pass will have the top priority. As with any other formation, if the running game takes priority, the stunts are called to the expected point of attack. Because this offense has a definite strong and weak side, the overshift may be used extensively against the pro formation.

The following combinations have been successfully used against the pro-type pass offense; "43, 3 cross in, middle fire at 3" (Diagram 7.15), "2 or 3 X to the split end" (Diagram 7.16), "jam the tight end and crash to the split end" (Diagram 7.17). "Over, double the split end, inside X back" (Diagram 7.18) is an example of a call which could be used if the split end is a special pass threat. The "blitz" call, as discussed in the preceding chapter, (Diagram 6.15) has also been effective against the pro offense.

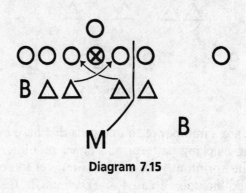

Diagram 7.15

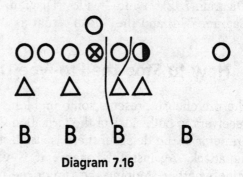

Diagram 7.16

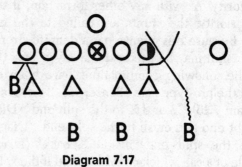

Diagram 7.17

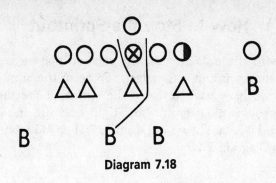

Diagram 7.18

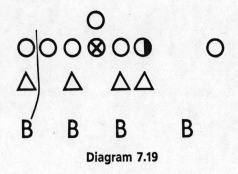

Diagram 7.19

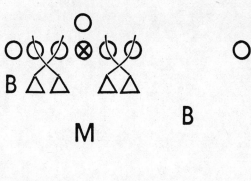

Diagram 7.20

How to Stop the Sprintout

As with the outside run, the rotation plays a key role in stopping the sprintout pass attack. Some of the stunting combinations we have used to force the sprintout are the "crash" stunt as shown in Diagram 7.8, "tight end fire in" (Diagram 7.19), "1 and 4 X" as shown in Diagram 7.11 or "43 rotate, 1 and 4 twist in" (Diagram 7.20).

8

STUNTING TO
STOP THE WISHBONE

The wishbone offense presents a problem to any defense. The wishbone is a balanced set but can attack with an overload to either side. Also, the counter dive or counter option will keep the defense from reacting too quickly to the initial flow of the play.

Stunting from the Even Front to Stop the Wishbone

Diagram 8.1 shows the 44 alignment against the wishbone formation. When in the basic alignment, the inside linebackers key the near halfback with responsibility for the dive or counter

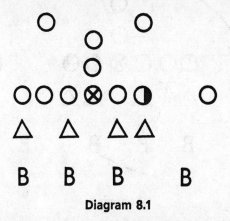

Diagram 8.1

dive as shown in Diagram 8.2. If the halfback moves to attack the corner, as in the lead option, the inside linebacker scrapes to help stop the inside option to the fullback while the inside linebacker away from the flow pursues (Diagram 8.3).

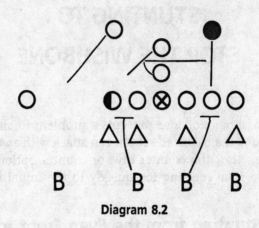

Diagram 8.2

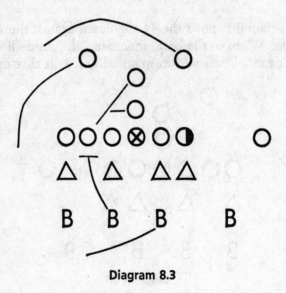

Diagram 8.3

The ends and outside linebackers are responsible for the outside option. We commit one of these defenders to the quarterback, while the other gets penetration and covers the pitchout. When not stunting, the end must tackle the quarterback or force the pitchout as soon as possible. We want the quarterback to commit himself as early as possible so the rest of the defensive team can react to the ball. These responsibilities may change based on the defensive call.

Two examples of changing the responsibilities would be: "crash to the split end" (Diagram 8.4) where the linebacker forces the quarterback and the end covers the pitchout, and "tight end fire in" (Diagram 8.5) when the responsibilities are again switched. Other stunts from the basic defense are "tackles stack out" (Diagram 8.6), "2 and 3 gap out, tight end gap in" (Diagram 8.7) or "odd or even X to the tight end" (Diagram 8.8).

The basic pass coverage is used against the wishbone. We feel the rotation gives excellent support on the outside option. The safeties rotate if, after taking their three shuffle steps, the ball is moving to the tackle. The outside safety moving into the flat will be in position to help make the tackle, along with the linebacker, on the halfback. As he rotates, the safety must know where the ball is. If the quarterback should get by the defensive

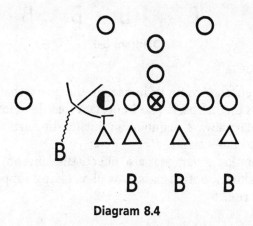

Diagram 8.4

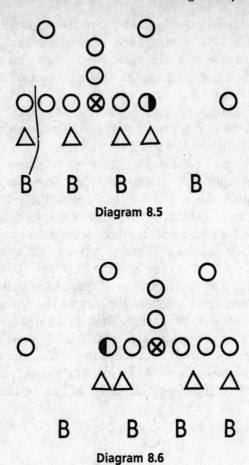

Diagram 8.5

Diagram 8.6

end, the linebacker commits himself to the quarterback, and the safety covers the halfback. It is important that the safety, rotating up to the play, always maintain an outside-in relationship with any potential ball carrier.

The rotating coverage is also effective against any deep play action or halfback option pass as well as giving support against the outside run.

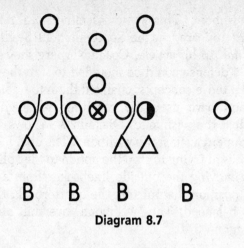

Diagram 8.7

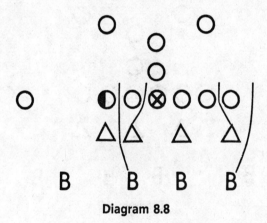

Diagram 8.8

Adjusting the Odd Alignment to Stop the Wishbone

As indicated earlier, the wishbone is a balanced offensive set. Therefore, unless a team has some very strong tendencies, there seems to be little advantage to overshifting the defense against the wishbone. This was our feeling, until an article by Greg Norberg appeared in the September, 1978 edition of the *Athletic Journal*. In his article, Coach Norberg showed how the standard 5-2-4 defense could be modified to stop the wishbone. We have taken these concepts, changed them to fit our overshift alignment, and have used the resulting 5-2 alignment successfully against the wishbone. Diagram 8.9 shows the normal overshift alignment against the wishbone. The obvious weakness of the defense is in trying to stop the option to the split end side. However, by moving the outside linebacker from a "monster" position to a position that mirrors the quarterback, the defense will become balanced. The "wishbone" overshift alignment is shown in Diagram 8.10.

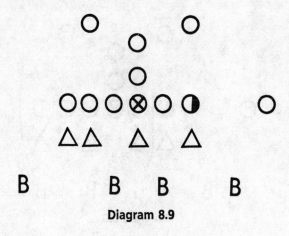

Diagram 8.9

Because our overshift alignment uses a defensive end on the tight end side and a linebacker on the split end side, we have found it convenient to flip-flop the entire defense when playing against the wishbone. This allows for the linemen to maintain their same relative position as the tight end goes to either side. The flexibility built into the basic defense allows for this movement with very little difficulty. As the offense breaks the

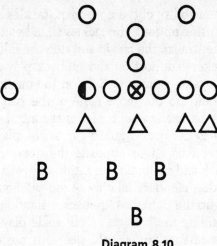

Diagram 8.10

huddle, the defensive unit looks for the tight end. The defensive end and front side tackle go with the tight end, while the nose man (the other tackle) and backside end go to the split end's side. The same outside linebacker always goes to the split end side while the other mirrors the quarterback.

The end and the outside linebacker are responsible for taking away the pitchout. On the snap of the ball, they get depth to prevent the quarterback from pitching out to the halfback. The end must first hold up the tight end for two counts so that the tight end cannot block the linebacker behind the nose man. The objective of the end or linebacker is to have the quarterback see him and not make the pitch. In order to be successful, the end or the linebacker will have to defeat the block of the lead halfback. This must be done by using the inside shoulder to shed the block and by getting into the quarterback's line of sight. We feel that, in most cases, the quarterback is less of a run threat than the halfback. The men who play the end and linebacker positions must also be agile enough to stay with the halfback as he turns the corner to prevent a last second pitchout. If the flow is away, the end or linebacker will contain.

The first responsibility of the nose man, tackles and inside linebackers is the inside option. The tackles align head up on the offensive tackles, neutralize the tackle and stop the fullback play. The inside linebackers support on the fullback play and, once they are sure it is a fake, pursue to help on the outside option. The nose man should be the more agile of the two defensive tackles when in the basic alignment. He must control the center and be able to get to the center-guard gap to the play side.

The linebacker who aligns opposite the quarterback mirrors the quarterback and maintains an inside-out relationship to him. As the outside defenders take away the pitchout and the quarterback turns up the field, the linebacker should tackle him just as if he were filling the hole on an off tackle play. The best tackler among the linebackers should play this position. Diagram 8.11 shows the defense against the outside play to the tight end, while the option to the split end is shown in Diagram 8.12.

This variation gives the defense a balanced front and will force the quarterback to run rather than make the pitchout. It

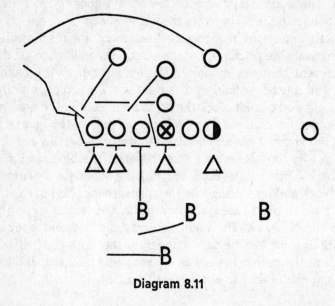

Diagram 8.11

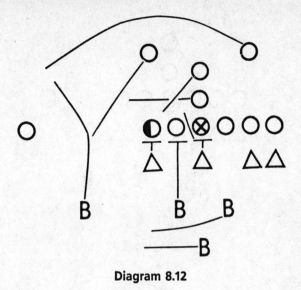

Diagram 8.12

has proven to be an excellent complement to our basic defense in stopping the wishbone attack. To prevent the offense from learning the responsibilities of the defenders, there are two change up calls that may be used. "Tackle switch" (Diagram 8.13) tells the linebacker and tackles to "switch" responsibilities. The tackles gap out to cut off the quarterback, and the linebacker fills the guard tackle gap to the play side, stopping the inside option. "End switch" (Diagram 8.14) involves the end and outside linebacker coming down the line to cut off the quarterback while the linebacker gets outside to cut off the pitchout.

How to Stop the Wishbone on the Goal Line

The problems presented by the wishbone become more critical in goal line situations. The defense must be balanced and

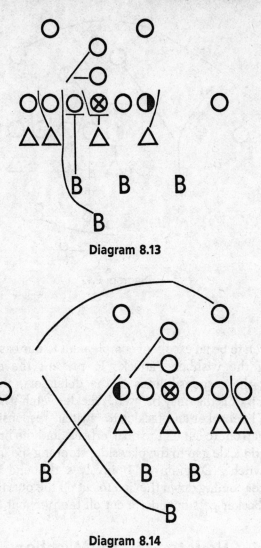

Diagram 8.13

Diagram 8.14

yet must be able to move quickly to the point of attack. Our goal line defense against the wishbone is a hybrid of the 6-5 along with our 5-2 wishbone defense. The alignment of this defense for the wishbone is shown in Diagram 8.15.

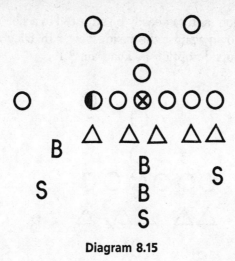

Diagram 8.15

The alignment and responsibilities of the four interior linemen are the same as the normal 6-5 goal line defense. The end and outside linebacker have the same responsibilities as they do in the overshift defense against the wishbone as discussed earlier in this chapter.

The unique characteristic of the defense is the stack, consisting of two linebackers and a safety, aligned on the center. The linebacker closer to the line of scrimmage keys the fullback. He is responsible for the inside option and filling the hole on any power play. The second linebacker mirrors the quarterback, having the same responsibilities as in the middle of the field overshift defense against the wishbone. The safety covers the halfback to the side of the play. This safety also adjusts to any wing or slot formation as shown in Diagrams 8.16 and 8.17.

The end and outside linebacker are still responsible for the pitchout and must cover that back, should he flare. The outside safeties play man to man coverage on the ends as in the normal goal line defense.

This defense allows for the maximum number of people to be at the point of attack, is flexible enough to defend both sides of the formation, and can easily be adjusted to a slot or wing. The defense is shown against the inside power in Diagram 8.18 and against the outside option in Diagram 8.19.

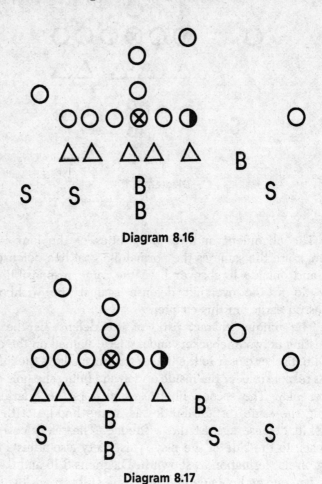

Diagram 8.16

Diagram 8.17

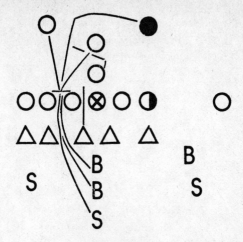

Diagram 8.18

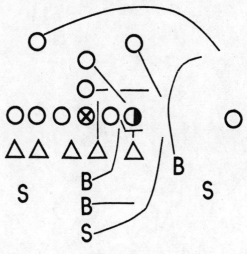

Diagram 8.19

9

USING MULTIPLE ALIGNMENTS IN GOAL LINE SITUATIONS

Much of our overall success on defense can be attributed to our goal line and short yardage defenses. We work very hard on these areas and spend a considerable amount of practice time defending short yardage and goal line situations. Our players accept these challenges and have changed the momentum of many games by stopping the opposition in a critical fourth down or on the goal line.

Personnel Selection for the Goal Line Defense

Our basic goal line alignment is a five man front with two linebackers and four safeties. The linemen consist of the five best defensive linemen on the squad, usually the starting four defensive linemen with another defensive tackle. The most agile of the tackles plays on the center, while the other tackles align in the guard-tackle gaps with the ends playing head up on a normal end.

The two most aggressive linebackers, who are also excellent tacklers, play on the goal line unit. When the defense changes from the 5-2 alignment to a 6-5, one of the linebackers becomes a defensive guard, so quickness is also important. When in the 5-2 alignment, the linebackers stack behind the tackles. The 5-2 alignment is shown in Diagram 9.1. Diagram 9.2 shows the movement to the 6-5; the 6-5 front is shown in Diagram 9.3.

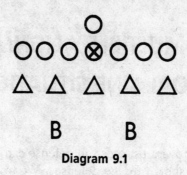

Diagram 9.1

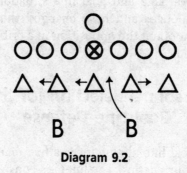

Diagram 9.2

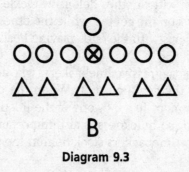

Diagram 9.3

The four safeties are picked on their ability to play man to man pass coverage along with their ability to fill the hole on a running play. The priority, however, is on pass coverage. Each of the safeties is assigned a man to cover. The man to man assignments vary from week to week so that the best defender will cover the most dangerous receiver. We feel this gives the defense much more flexibility when compared to a system that uses a left safety and right safety regardless of the offensive formation. By assigning defenders to a specific receiver, the offense cannot gain an advantage by changing formations from one side to the other.

Adjusting the Goal Line Defense to Any Formation

The system of assigning each safety a man to cover gives the defense a great deal of flexibility in adjusting to any offensive formation. The safeties align themselves so they can best cover their assigned man. Those responsible for the ends adjust their alignment as the end splits, while the safeties who are covering the halfbacks mirror the alignment of the backs. The fullback is the responsibility of the linebacker in the 6-5 or linebackers in the 5-2.

We feel there are a number of advantages in having the alignment of the defenders determined by the offense. These advantages are: the defense can easily adjust to any spread or "triple" formation we might see, the best pass defender always covers the best receiver regardless of where he is aligned, and the safeties are in a good position to fill the hole and support on the inside running game. Diagram 9.4 shows the 5-2 alignment against a wide slot; the alignment of our 6-5 is shown against a triple in Diagram 9.5; Diagram 9.6 shows the 6-5 alignment against a pro set; Diagrams 9.7 and 9.8 show the 5-2 goal line against a wing and the 6-5 against a full house back field respectively.

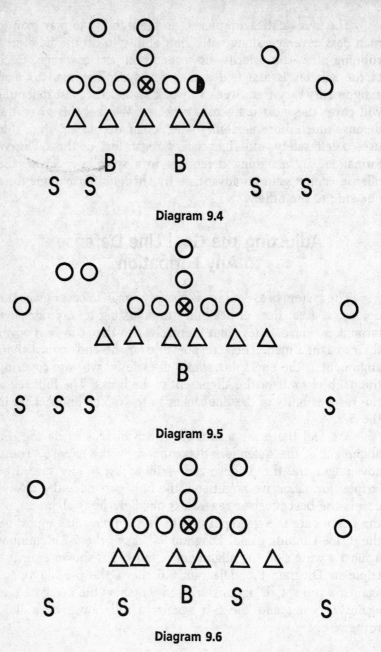

Diagram 9.4

Diagram 9.5

Diagram 9.6

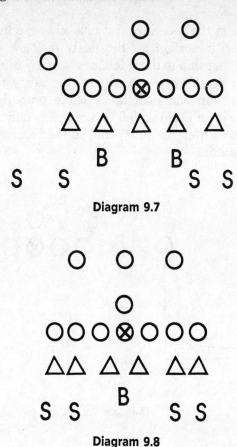

Diagram 9.7

Diagram 9.8

Playing Pass Defense on the Goal Line

All goal line pass defense is man to man. As indicated in the preceding section, the defenders are assigned specific receivers to cover on a week to week basis. On the goal line it is critical that the receivers not be allowed a quick inside release. The safety must be aware that, in the goal line alignments, there is no inside help from the linebackers. The closer the receiver aligns to the sideline, the more aware the safety must be of the quick slant-in pass. Therefore, in goal line situations, the safeties align on the inside of the receivers and take away the inside release first. It is also important for the safety to know where he is aligned in relationship to the sideline, so he may use the sideline as an aide in playing pass defense. If the safety maintains an inside relationship and uses the sideline properly, the "out" pattern as shown in Diagram 9.9 becomes very difficult. The ball must be thrown over the safety and to the receiver while still staying in bounds.

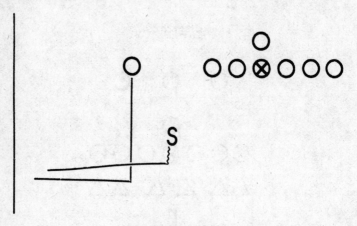

Diagram 9.9

Playing pass defense in the end zone is much different from playing pass defense in the middle of the field. Our defenders are taught that in the middle of the field the receiver must not get behind him. If the pass is well thrown, we would rather have the pass caught in front of the safety for a gain as compared to behind the safety for a touchdown. When playing pass defense in the end zone, it is essential that the defender be between the quarterback and receiver when the ball is thrown. This is similar to man to man defense as played in basketball, where the defender must stay between his man and the ball. The "man on man end zone drill" as shown in Chapter 11 is used to work on this coverage.

It does not help the defense if the ball is caught in front of the safety, in the end zone, and the safety then makes the tackle. When the receiver makes his cut, in the end zone, the safeties are taught to move in *front* of the receiver. We expect our defender to make a legitimate attempt as the ball is in the air, to get to the ball with his body between the ball and the receiver. Again, the sidelines and end line must become a "friend" to the defender in these situations.

It is important to note that the pass coverage is dependent on the rush generated by the defensive front. If a receiver has time to make two or three "moves" in the end zone, the fault, if the offense scores, is in the pass rush and not the coverage.

How To Stop the Inside Power Running Game

The use of two alignments in goal line situations allows us to choose the defense that is best suited to stop the offense we will face that particular week. We determine, each week at our scouting meeting, which alignment we will use for the upcoming game. There are times when we use both the 5-2 and 6-5 in the same game based on down and distance or formation tendencies. We feel that the 6-5 alignment is more advantageous in stopping the inside run and the off tackle power play. Whenever the offense uses, what we believe to be, a power formation, we shift from the 5-2 to the 6-5 as shown in Diagrams 9.2 and 9.3.

Note that inside the three yard line, the 6-5 alignment is almost always used, as we feel the nose tackle in the 5-2 alignment cannot properly defend both center-guard gaps against the quarterback sneak. The responsibility of stopping the "sneak" is shared by the two guards in the 6-5 alignment.

In the 6-5 alignment, the guards align in the center-guard gap and penetrate as quickly as possible. They must not allow themselves to be piled up in the center and should chase the play if it goes away.

The tackles line up on the head of the offensive tackle and while not picking a side, the tackle neutralizes the offensive tackle with a blow from his outside arm. The first responsibility of the defensive tackle is the inside dive hole. It is important that the tackle not get blocked down to the center by the offensive tackle. The defender must fight through the blocker as he gets penetration.

The ends align on the head of a normal end and make any formation adjustment that is necessary. The end must hold up the offensive end with his *inside* arm. The offensive end cannot be given a free release for a quick pass, and the inside arm must be used because the end has the contain responsibility in the goal line defense. Any time the play goes away from the end, he cannot chase or pursue. The end must stay in position for a reverse or counter. This is a goal line situation and by the time the end catches the play, the ball will most likely be in the end zone.

The linebacker in the 6-5 is responsible for the fullback. He mirrors the fullback's alignment and fills the hole if the fullback moves into the line or covers him if the fullback releases on a pass. Diagram 9.10 shows the 6-5 alignment against the fullback power from the wing formation, while the off tackle power play from an "I" formation is shown in Diagram 9.11. The linebacker and safeties are responsible for filling the hole and tackling in such a way that the ball carrier is pushed backwards. In fact, we emphasize the second and third man in on any tackle should be working to push the ball carrier backwards and trying to cause a fumble in all defensive situations.

The six down linemen along with the flexibility afforded by our match up man to man coverage in the secondary allows us to get a lot of people to the point of attack against the run without sacrificing the pass coverage.

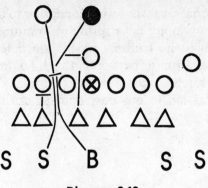

Diagram 9.10

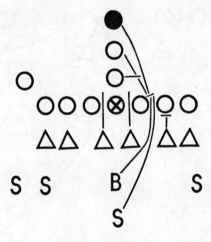

Diagram 9.11

How to Stop the Sprintout or Rollout Attack

At one time, the 6-5 was our only goal line defense. However, we have found that when the offense spread out and attacked the corner we were weakened, due to our man to man coverage. For example, on a sprintout toward a slot formation (Diagram 9.12) if the halfback blocks the defensive end, the quarterback has a run or pass option with no pressure from the defense as the safeties *must* stay with their man. This is the type of situation that led to our development of the 5-2 goal line defense.

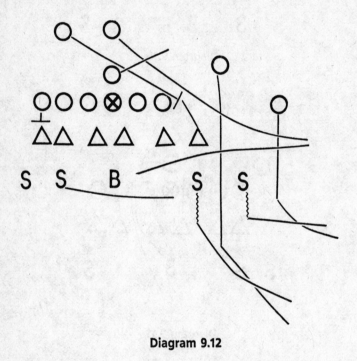

Diagram 9.12

From the 5-2 alignment which is shown in Diagram 9.1, the tackles will close down through the outside shoulder of the guard. The end, if the flow is coming to him, will, after holding up the offensive end, close down the off tackle hole or cut off the quarterback on a sprintout. If the flow is away, the end will stay in position to contain.

The linebackers react to the flow of the play. The linebacker to the play side moves to the outside of the end and helps pressure the quarterback. The linebacker away from the flow becomes responsible for the fullback. Diagram 9.13 shows the advantage of the 5-2 alignment in defending the sprintout as compared to the 6-5 in Diagram 9.12. The 5-2 goal line has also been successful against the outside run with the end forcing the play, and the linebacker containing and forcing the ball back into the pursuit.

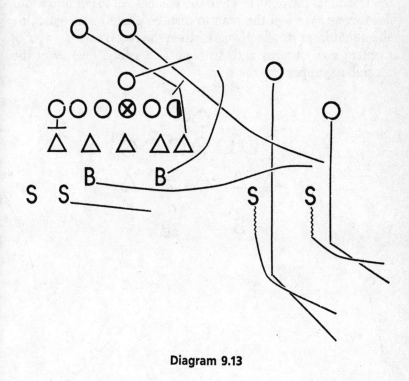

Diagram 9.13

The change between the 6-5 and the 5-2 does not affect the safeties or the pass coverage in any way.

How to Use the Goal Line Defense in Normal Short Yardage Situations

We have been successful in using the goal line defense in short yardage situations when the offense is in a four down zone. As stated at the beginning of this chapter, we enjoy the challenge of stopping a team on third and fourth down. However, because of the man to man coverage, we have been reluctant to use the goal line defense on third down and short yardage situations in the middle of the field or when the ball has yet to get into a four down zone. We feel the man to man coverage in the goal line alignment loses its effectiveness when the receivers have a lot of room to run patterns and, with no free safety, take away the secondary support on the run.

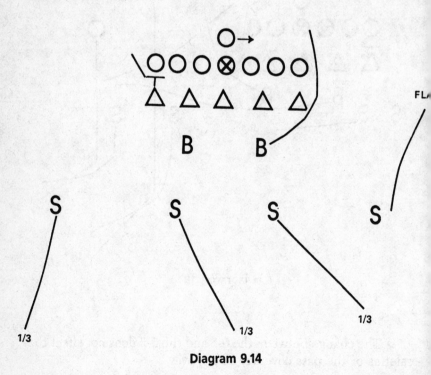

Diagram 9.14

When we developed our 4-3 pass coverages, as discussed in Chapter 6, we found the solution to our problem. By using the 4-3 zone pass coverage along with the 5-2 or 6-5 goal line front alignment, we have a combination to stop the short yardage play in the three down zone. The front five and linebackers play the defense exactly the same way as on the goal line. The safeties align as they do in the 4-3 zone defense. As with the 4-3 zone, the rotation is to a predetermined key, which usually is the flow of the play or the strength of the formation. The rotation of the defense as shown in Diagram 9.14 will be the same as in the 4-3 zone.

The zone coverage is called in the huddle. If there is no coverage call, the goal line defense is always man to man.

10

PREPARING FOR THE GAME USING THE STUNTING DEFENSE

The Importance of the Scouting Meeting

Our defensive program has so many alignments and stunts available to choose from that it is neither advisable nor even realistic to use them all in any one game. Therefore, it is up to the coaching staff to determine, on a week to week basis, which variations will give us the best advantage for that specific opponent. Several times in the preceding chapters reference has been made to the weekly scouting meeting. It is at this meeting that the preliminary defensive game plan is drafted. The information gathered by our scout provides the primary source of information used in determining which defensive alignments and stunts will be used.

In our system, each team is scouted for two weeks before we play them. The scout charts every play the team runs in those two games. The information included for each play is down and distance, formation, point of attack, ball carrier and, if possible, type of blocking. On the scouting form, two charts are extremely important in determining the defensive game plan. They are the Down and Distance chart (Diagram 10.1) and the Formation Tendency Chart (Diagram 10.2).

These charts, when the information they contain is broken down, either by use of the Defensive Frequency Chart (Diagram 10.4 or 10.5) for down and distance or by inspection for formations, will help the coaches to determine whether the

DOWN AND DISTANCE CHART

1st		2nd			3rd			4th	Key
10+	10	8+	6-4	3-0	5+	4-3	2-0		
									1. = QB
									2. = RHB
									3. = LHB
									4. = FB

Diagram 10.1

122

FORMATION TENDENCY CHART

formation

1	2	3	4	5	6	7	8	9

Diagram 10.2

upcoming opponent has stronger tendencies based on the formations they use or on the down and yards to gain.

If there has been no change in the opposition's coach, last year's film is again analyzed and last year's Defensive Call Sheet (see Diagram 10.3) is checked to see if there are any noticeable changes in that team's offensive philosophy. This information is compared to the current tendencies shown on the scouting report and the game plan is then formulated. When the current tendencies vary from the past, we base our planning on what the opposition is now doing. If during the course of the game they go back to their past tendencies, our program is flexible enough so that the appropriate adjustments can be made.

How to Use "Automatic" Defenses

The call sheet shown in Diagram 10.3 is designed for a team which shows tendencies based on down and yards to gain. Sometimes, during the course of a season, we find a team which shows very strong tendencies to run specific plays from certain formations. When this occurs, we consider using an "automatic" defense against that formation. This would be similar to an adjustment made by teams using a more standard defense to a specific formation. The primary difference is the number of possibilities we have to choose from, as the "automatic" defense may be an alignment change and/or stunt that will be used every time the offense is in that formation.

When using "automatic" defenses, it is very important that the opposition not become aware of what the defense is doing. The defense should not use words like "special" or "automatic" in these situations. Our experience has shown that association of the "automatic" defense with the name of the formation has been most successful. That is, as the linebackers call out the formation, which they do every play, the defense will associate the name of the formation with the "automatic" defense.

DEFENSIVE CALL SHEET

situation	tendency	defenses
1-10+		
1-10		
2-long (8+)		
2-normal (5-7)		
2-short (1-5)		
3-long (4+)		
3-normal		
4th		

Diagram 10.3

DEFENSIVE FREQUENCY CHART

	PASS	1	2	3	4	5	6	7	8	9	formation to _away_
1-10+											
1-10											
2-8+											
2-(5-7)											

	PASS		NOTES:
	dropback	sprintout or rollout to away	
2-(1-4)			
3-4+			
3-(1-3)			
4th			

Diagram 10.4

How to Prepare the Defensive Call Sheet

The Defensive Call Sheet (Diagram 10.3) is prepared from the information obtained by breaking down the Down and Distance Chart (Diagram 9.1) section of the scouting report. By taking the plays listed in each category and using one of the charts shown in Diagram 10.4 or Diagram 10.5, it is possible to determine the frequency which the offense runs at each hole. The chart shown in Diagram 10.4 is numbered to be consistent with our offensive system so that, during the development of the call sheet, the coaches are all using the same point of reference. "To" and "Away" in Diagram 10.5 refer to the tight end.

After the overall tendencies and frequency of attack have been determined, the staff then chooses the defenses which, we feel, will best be able to neutralize the offense in each given situation. We would try to use both the basic and overshift variations, if applicable, in the same down and distance category so as to constantly vary the defensive front. This reliance on tendencies has proven successful for us. Most teams will not change drastically from the previous two weeks and, if they do, we have the flexibility to adjust as will be discussed later in this chapter. Diagram 10.6 shows a completed defensive call sheet for a hypothetical opponent.

How to Call the Defensive Signals

Once the defensive game plan has been prepared, there are two schools of thought as to how these defenses should be called in the game. There are those who have the defensive captain make the calls. However, we feel with the wide number of variations, stunts and pass coverages available, this puts a lot of extra pressure on that individual. It is also difficult for someone who is playing in the game to become aware of changes in the

WISHBONE
DEFENSIVE FREQUENCY CHART

	inside option to / away	outside option to / away	power to / away	counter	pass
1–10+					
1–10					
2–8+					
2–(5–7)					
2–(1–4)					
3–4+					
3–(1–3)					
4th					

Diagram 10.5

NOTES:

DEFENSIVE CALL SHEET

situation	tendency	defenses
1–10+		
1–10	32 plays 6 pass 26 run <u>23</u> between tackles 26	2,3 wide—1,4 gap in 2,3 tight—2,3 gap out over—double stack over—double eagle under TE fire
2-long (8+)	9 pass 8 run 5 run our right side <u>draw</u>	3X TE gap in—2,3 gap out over, eagle right, inside X right
2-normal (5–7)	2 pass 6 run <u>5</u> 6 run our right	under, 3 fire over, nose right over stack right, inside X right 2,3 tight—tackles stack out jam right guard

2-short (1–5)	2 run inside	LB's tight 4–3 over, all gap in
3-long (4+)	8 pass 5 run (no tendency) may quick kick	4–3 blitz 4–3 crash SE 4–3 double SE over, crash SE
3–normal	5 run $\frac{4}{5}$ our right, inside 2 pass	tackles stack in jam right guard over, stack right, inside X right 5–2 rotate
4th	1 pass 1 run	also: goal line—6–5 4–3 prevent

Diagram 10.6

131

pattern or tendencies of the offense. For example, in our situation, the defensive captain will probably play both offense and defense, which will make it difficult for the coaches to communicate any changes to him. We would rather have the players concentrate on execution and call the defensive signals from the sideline. As each defensive call is made, we have a substitute player chart the call so that the coaches know what defense is being used on each play when the game films are evaluated.

It is important to understand that field position plays an important part in determining which specific call is used. Our statistics show that the longer the distance the offense has to go, 60 to 70 yards for example, the lower their chances are of scoring. However, if the offense gets the ball only 30 yards away from our goal line, their chances of scoring increase dramatically. With this in mind, the defensive coach might vary from the call sheet in order to force some kind of mistake by the offense. The "blitz" call as shown in Diagram 6.15 is a good example. These are some examples of why we feel it is advantageous to call the defensive signals from the sideline as compared with having the signals called by the defensive captain.

Once it has been decided that the coaches will call the signals, either of two systems may be used based on the preference of the coaching staff. The defenses may be indicated to the captain by a series of hand signals or by means of a player shuttle system.

Regardless of how the defenses are called, it is important that the players, especially the linemen and linebackers, be able to communicate with each other before the offense has set. If, for example, an "X" stunt has been called, the lineman and linebacker must communicate as to who is going in each direction (remember—the linebacker tells the lineman). A stunt that involves the outside units could mean the contain responsibility might have to be changed. These are only two situations in which communication after the defensive call but before the play is important. To facilitate this communication, the defensive huddle is arranged so that the linemen and their respective linebackers are close to each other. This huddle is shown in Diagram 10.7.

DEFENSIVE HUDDLE

4LB   RS   MS   LS   1LB

4E   3T   3LB   2T   1E

2LB

The positions of the 2 and 3 LB's are interchangeable depending on the personnel.

Diagram 10.7

Planning the Defensive Practice

As indicated in the introduction to this book, we do not get a large turnout for our football program. Over the last eight years, our squad has averaged between forty and forty-five young men. This includes sophomores through seniors. As a result, many of our better athletes play both offense and defense, which limits the amount of practice time we can devote to either area.

When the regular season starts, we have a three day work week. The varsity games are played on Saturday afternoons and the J.V. game is played Monday after school. Because of the J.V. games, we have approximately fifteen to twenty boys for practice Monday. Therefore, Mondays are used for film evaluation, endurance type conditioning and strength training. Tuesday, Wednesday and Thursday are used as the work days for each week with a very light workout on Friday.

The workouts on Tuesday, Wednesday and Thursday are split evenly between offense and defense. Usually Tuesday is our defensive day, Wednesday is spent on offense and Thursday is divided evenly into defense, offense and the kicking game. Also, Thursday practices are all team work while on Tuesday and Wednesday individual and group drills are emphasized.

Diagram 10.8 shows a typical defensive practice plan. At the end of their classes, the football players have approximately 15 minutes of free time before the pre-practice meeting. From the start of the meeting, there are three (3) hours until the departure of the late buses. Due to the bus schedule, (70% of the student body rides buses), and because we demand a maximum effort during practice, the actual on the field practice will rarely exceed two (2) hours. The schedule shown in Diagram 10.8 allows twenty minutes for dressing before and after practice along with a fifteen minute meeting which leaves two hours and five minutes for the actual practice time.

While the total time for practice stays the same, the time given for any segment may be changed as the coaches see the need. For example, in the pre-season, when the defensive alignments and stunts are first taught; the meeting and group run time is extended with a corresponding decrease in the time for team work. There are only three coaches working with the squad so that one coach is with each group throughout the individual and group phases of practice. The specific drills we use will be discussed in Chapter 11.

Adjusting the Defensive Plan During the Game

When the game begins, it is possible that the opposition might change from the expected tendencies. This may be an effort on their part to take advantage of a weakness they feel exists in the defensive personnel, or it may be due to the weather, field conditions, the score of the game, or a number of other possibilities. To anticipate this possibility, we have one of our substitute players chart each play, using the appropriate frequency chart (Diagrams 10.4 and 10.5). The defensive coach has this chart available, during the game, and refers to it whenever he feels the offense is doing something other than what was expected.

The defense is *not* limited to the calls on the Defensive Call Sheet. This sheet is only a guideline as to what combinations might be used. One of the greatest advantages of our defensive program is its flexibility. It is possible, when necessary, to change the entire look and thrust of the defense without having to make any "major" adjustments. Once the players know what their key words mean, the defensive combinations may easily be changed to meet any changes the opposition may try.

DEFENSIVE PRACTICE PLAN

MEETING: (15 min.)

—offensive tendencies of opponents
—special plays
—automatic defenses, if used
—pass coverages
—goal line situations

SPECIALITIES: (10 min.)

Kickers, kick returners, quarterbacks throw, LB pass drops, interception drills, etc. Front work on stunt techniques

FLEXIBILITIES: (20 min.)

INDIVIDUAL: (15 min.)

Front	LB	Safeties
sled work	agility work	zone drops
work on basic techniques	shed drills	ball
work on stunt techniques	tackling drills	individual drills

GROUP (run): (15 min.)

Front & LB
Read drills
(inside and outside
units react to keys)

Safeties
Rotation drills
Sideline tackling
Goal line coverage

GROUP (pass): (15 min.)

Front
Pass rush drills

LB & Safeties
Skeleton pass
Defense vs. scout offense

KICKING: (10 min.)

2 phases of kicking game, usually punt return and kickoff

TEAM: (25 min.)

Team defense vs. scout offense. Be sure to use hash marks. Use call sheet as guideline. Last 10 minutes—goal line

CONDITIONING: (15 min.)

Running to be determined by coaches along with strength maintenance weight lifting program (½ each day).

Diagram 10.8

11

DRILLS FOR TEACHING
THE STUNTING DEFENSE

The drills we use for teaching and improving our players are not unique. I'm sure that many of these drills are already being used in your program. These drills are simple to execute, and each has a specific purpose. We do not believe in doing drills just to do drills.

The actual drills which are used on a given day will vary during the pre-season and also will change from week to week during the season depending on the strengths of our opponent. Please remember, we use the pre-season primarily to teach all of our alignments, coverages and stunts. We emphasize work on specific skills during scrimmages and the actual season.

Individual Drills for the Linemen

As you read this section on drills for the linemen, it is important to emphasize the role of quickness and aggressiveness in the success of our stunting defense. We firmly believe that concentration and desire can make an athlete quick and that speed and quickness are not the same. We drill and emphasize quickness in our defensive team from the first day of practice.

Beat the Blocker

This drill is done for quickness. The defensive linemen form two lines facing each other. The coach is positioned behind one of the lines. The line with their backs to the coach are the defenders. The coach gives the offense a hand signal as to when the ball is to be snapped. On the snap, the defender must get off on the ball and deliver a blow to control the blocker. It is critical that the defender remain parallel to the line of scrimmage.

In this drill, we emphasize the use of a forearm shiver combined with a hand shiver. Quickness and remaining parallel to the line of scrimmage must also be emphasized. The alignment for "Beat the Blocker" is shown in Diagram 11.1

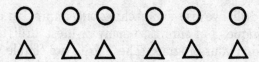

C

Diagram 11.1

Stunt Drill

This drill is used to teach the proper technique for the three stunts that involve only the linemen (gap, slant, cross). The alignment for the drill is the same as shown in Diagram 11.1. When doing this drill, the coach will tell the defenders to execute one of the three stunts before giving the offense the snap count. On the snap, the defenders must execute the stunt. Again quickness and remaining parallel to the line of scrimmage are the key coaching points.

We execute these stunts by having our linemen take an open step in the direction of the stunt. We feel the crossover step makes it difficult to maintain a good hitting position when stunting. After reaching the aiming point (one yard penetration) the defender must be in a good hitting position and ready to make the tackle. On all stunts, we teach our players to expect the ball to be coming at them and to be ready to make the tackle.

Piano Drills

The "piano" drills refer to a series of drills done using the seven man sled. These drills include the two hand shiver, forearm shiver, hit and spin, hit and sit, and the body extension. These drills are done in a series and emphasize delivering a solid blow along with quickness and agility.

The linemen form a single line about two yards in front of the first pad on the sled. On a signal from the coach, the first player delivers a two hand shiver to the pad, shuffles, delivers a two hand shiver to the second pad, and continues until he has hit all seven pads. When the first player has reached the third pad, the second starts. When all of the linemen have completed the drill, it is repeated so that everyone works his way back to the original starting point. The forearm shiver drill is done the same way with the inside arm being used to deliver the blow and "lift" the sled.

The "hit and spin" section of the "piano drills" emphasizes balance as the lineman delivers a blow with the inside shoulder, recoils (staying on his feet), spins and repeats the drill on every other pad (1st, 3rd, 5th, 7th). This drill is done down and back as are all these drills. The path of this drill is shown in Diagram 11.2.

The "hit and sit" drill involves the lineman hitting into the sled with his inside shoulder from a three point stance, dropping his "tail" to the ground as he turns his back to the sled (sitting), and recovering in a good position to hit the next pad. Every pad is used in this drill.

The "body extension" requires a full extension of the body exploding into the sled from the hands and knees. The lineman will then shuffle to the next pad, recoil and explode into that pad. Again, each pad is used both down and back.

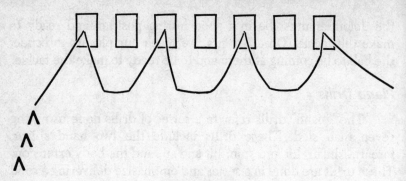

Diagram 11.2

Double Team Drill

Diagram 11.3 shows the alignment for the "double team" drill. The coach, by using a series of hand signals, indicates the blocking pattern and snap count to the offense. On the snap, the defender must defeat the man on his head and react to any double team pressure. The defender must not be caved in or moved backward. If he should start to be moved in either of those directions, he must go to the ground and make a pile at the point of attack. If the defender causes a pile to be made on "their" side of the neutral zone, he has done his job. As always, quickness is emphasized. We must "play" on the offensive side of the line of scrimmage.

Diagram 11.3

Pass Rush Drill

Whenever our linemen are not stunting, their first responsibility is to neutralize the blocker in front of them. As stated earlier in this section we prefer a forearm and hand shiver combination to accomplish this task. After the blocker has been controlled, if the play is a pass, the lineman must use his hands to get rid of the blocker and rush the quarterback. This drill is set up as shown in Diagram 11.1 with the coach giving the count to the offense. When doing this drill, we also emphasize getting the hands up to distract the quarterback. We sometimes get a manager or one of our "walking wounded' to stand in the quarterback position and have the linemen go by him with their hands up.

Individual Drills for the Linebacker

As is the case with many defensive schemes, our linebackers are very important to the overall success of our defense. In many of our stunts we expect the linemen to vacate an area and then bring the linebacker to the expected point of attack. Therefore, most of our individual linebacker drills deal with shedding blockers and tackling. Both the shed drills and tackling drills are taught in a progression, with the final step of the progression emphasized during our in-season, individual defensive work. The linebacker pass responsibility will be covered in our group pass drills that are discussed later in this chapter.

Shed Drills

The ability of the linebacker to shed blockers is critical to the success of our defense. Whether filling a hole or pursuing, the linebacker must be able to defeat the blocker before he can make the tackle. Our linebackers work on shedding the straight ahead block, the high cut off block and the roll or cut block. The drill for each type of shed technique starts the same way as shown in Diagram 11.4, for eventually the linebacker will have to be able to react to the blocker, not knowing what type of block to expect.

B

C

Diagram 11.4

To defeat the straight ahead block, the linebacker must stay square. If the linebacker is going to use his right forearm to defeat the blocker, the contact must be with the blocker's left side. The linebacker must not turn his body. When the right forearm is used, the left hand is used to control and "throw" the blocker out of the way. When doing this or any of the shed drills, the linebacker sheds three blockers and gets into position to make the tackle on the fourth player in the line. When working on defeating the straight ahead block, it is very important that the linebacker not move either of his feet backwards. This becomes critical after contact is made and the linebacker is getting rid of the potential blocker.

Many players have a tendency to move one foot back as they "throw" the blocker away. We call this the "swinging door" and work very hard on correcting this mistake. Once the linebacker loses his parallel stance, he "opens the door" for the back to cut as he can now be screened by the blocker. The hit and "throw" of the blocker must be accomplished while maintaining a parallel stance and a good football position. Diagram 11.5 shows both the correct and incorrect foot positions for the linebacker when shedding the straight ahead block.

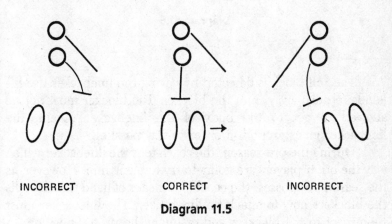

INCORRECT   CORRECT   INCORRECT

Diagram 11.5

The linebackers must also develop the ability to shed the cut off block. The key coaching point in defeating this type of block is to "keep the outside arm free." It doesn't matter whether one of the inside linebackers is pursuing the play or if one of the outside linebackers is defending the corner; the contact must be made with the inside arm on the outside of the blocker. Diagram 11.6 shows a linebacker shedding the cutoff block in our drills. The linebacker must not let the ball carrier get to the outside. He must force the play back into the pursuit or make the tackle himself if the back tries to get to the outside. The linebacker will give some ground, if necessary, but, as in the straight on block, the body and feet must remain parallel to the line of scrimmage.

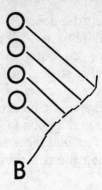

Diagram 11.6

The roll block is defeated by having the linebacker use his hands to push away from the blocker. The blocker must not be allowed to get to the body of the linebacker. Again, the linebacker gives ground in order to stay parallel.

During the pre-season, the coach tells the linebacker which way the other players are going to try to block him. However, as the season progresses, the coach, by means of hand signals, tells the blockers how to attack the linebacker. The linebacker must then react to the blockers and maintain the proper position.

Form Tackling

This is the first in a series of three tackling drills. The linebackers form two lines, facing each other, five yards apart. One line will be the tacklers, the other the ball carriers. On the coach's command, the lines move toward each other at half speed and the ball carrier allows himself to be tackled. This drill is done at half speed so that all of the techniques necessary for good tackling can be emphasized. These are: Keep the head up (put face mask on the ball), drop the hips, drive the hips (explode) into the ball carrier, pull the ball carrier in with clasped hands , lift (with the legs), and carry the ball carrier for five yards. This drill is done every defensive day until the coach is satisfied the linebackers can tackle properly. Sometimes, if we tackled poorly in a game, we go back to this drill during the season.

Scramble Tackling

When the coach is satisfied that the linebackers know the proper tackling technique, this drill is the next step in our progression. Each player has a partner. The players lie on their backs so that their bodies form a straight line with the top of their helmets touching. The coach designates one player as the ball carrier. On command, both players scramble to their feet and the ball carrier tries to run over the tackler. The tackler must quickly get to a good football position and, using good form, tackle the ball carrier. This drill emphasizes quickness and good tackling technique.

Fill the Hole Tackling

This is the last and most frequently used of our tackling drills. This drill emphasizes proper pursuit relationship, proper tackling form and the concept of attacking the ball carrier. The drill is set up as shown in Diagram 11.7, but it may be started on

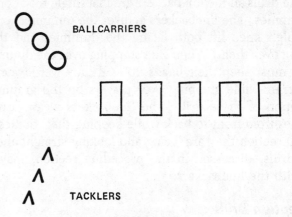

Diagram 11.7

either side of the dummies or in the middle. The players are approximately one yard from their end of the dummies at the start. The drill begins on the movement of the ball carrier. The tackler must maintain an inside-out relationship to the ball. When the ball carrier cuts between the bags, the linebacker must "fill the hole" by squaring up and "exploding" into the ball carrier using the proper form. The tackle must be made between the dummies, not on the defensive side of the dummies. The ball carrier may pick any hole he wishes and the linebacker must react to his movements. It is important to maintain the inside-out relationship as this will prevent over pursuit in a game situation.

The "fill the hole" tackling and "shed" drills are essential to successful linebacker play in a stunting defense. The linebackers must be able to avoid being blocked and be able to make the tackle in the offensive zone for the stunts to be successful.

Agility Drills

To complement the shed and tackling drills, a series of agility drills are done to improve quickness and lateral movement. A line of dummies is set up as shown in Diagram 11.7, but for these drills all the linebackers are in a single file at one end of the dummies. The linebackers go over the dummies, emphasizing a high knee lift both facing the dummies and then side stepping over them. When side stepping over the dummies, the players must keep their heads up as if they were watching the ball carrier while stepping over players on the ground. Upon completion of these drills, the linebackers weave around the dummies from front to back while keeping their bodies parallel to the direction they are facing and looking straight ahead. The piano drills, discussed in the preceding section, may also be used with the linebackers.

Interception Drills

During the specialty or pre-practice period of our defensive practices, the linebackers do a series of drills that we feel will help them to make an interception when the opportunity presents itself. There are four drills, and with two "quarterbacks" all can be easily done within the ten minute speciality period. The "High Point" and "Hot Potato" drills are done exactly as our safeties do them and are discussed in the next section. The third drill is a variation of the High Point drill in that the ball is thrown either to the right or left and the linebacker attempts to catch the ball. The fourth drill involves a lateral pass drop and a one handed catch by the linebacker. This drill is done to both sides. If time permits, we may also have two linebackers go up for the ball as discussed in the "Get to the Ball" drill for the safeties.

Individual Drills for the Safety

The drills we use with the safeties can be divided into three groups: pass coverage, tackling and ball handling. Each defensive day the coach picks the drills which are most appropriate for that practice based on the time of the season, the upcoming opponent or the techniques which were poorly executed in last week's game. Time does not allow for all the drills to be incorporated into a single practice session.

We use three drills in working on pass coverage with the safeties. They are: "Drop to Middle of Zone," "Rotation Drill" and the "Man on Man End Zone Drill."

Drop to Middle of Zone

This drill is done from the first day of practice. Three cones are set up to signify the middle of the three deep zones in our coverage. These cones are approximately 25 yards down field behind the safeties. The coach starts with the ball anywhere on or between the hash marks. On the snap, the safeties, while keeping their eyes on the coach, drop to the middle of the zone. After three seconds, the movement stops and the safeties check their alignment with the cones. It is extremely important that the area used for this drill be the standard width of a football field and that both hash marks are used. The safeties must know the importance of getting to the middle of their zone. This is a drop back pass drill.

As the players become proficient at dropping to the middle of their zones, a variation may be introduced by having receivers run patterns and making the safeties defend against the deep pass. Early in the season the coach must emphasize the importance of staying in the middle of the zone until the ball is released. Diagram 11.8 shows this drill with the ball on the defensive right hash mark.

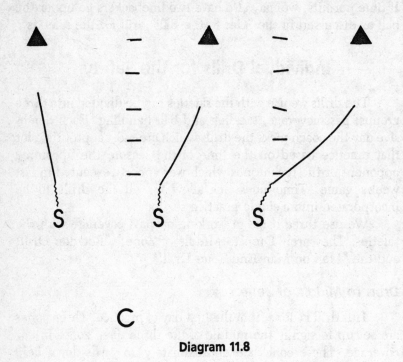

Diagram 11.8

Rotation Drill

The "Rotation Drill" is set up the same way as the "Drop to Middle of Zone" drill. Everything is the same except the coverage now involves our rotation. The safeties, after taking three steps toward the middle of their zones, locate the ball and rotate when the ball is moving to the tackle. Spare players or dummies are used to determine the position of the offensive tackles. The use of a field with the standard width and the use of the hash marks must again be emphasized. This drill is done with both the three deep and four deep rotation and may also be done with receivers. Diagram 11.9 shows the three deep rotation with the ball on the defensive left hash mark.

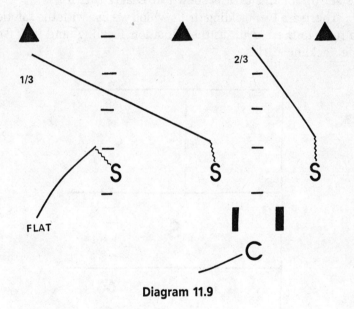

Diagram 11.9

Man on Man End Zone Drill

As the name indicates, this drill is done to improve our man on man coverage in goal line situations. As discussed in Chapter 9 the man on man in the end zone is played differently from the man on man in the middle of the field. The passer is set up on the hash mark at the seven yard line. The receiver tells the passer what route he will run. The defender aligns himself with his inside foot up as to take away the inside release and forces the receiver to the outside. As shown in Diagram 9.9, the defender must learn to use the sideline and end line as a friend and must play in front of the receiver. This will force the passer to throw over the defender and still keep the ball in bounds. The offense is restricted to a 10 yard box for the pattern and has a three second time limit for each pass. The hash mark will be changed so that the defenders will have to work both sides of the field. The set up for this drill is shown in Diagram 11.10.

There are two tackling drills which we use with the safeties. We refer to these drills as the "Rotation Tackling" and the "Goal Line Tackling" drills.

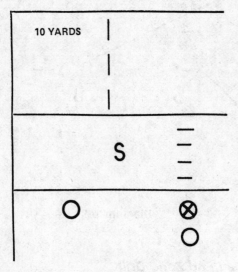

Diagram 11.10

Rotation Tackling

The "Rotation Tackling" drill is an extension of the "Rotation Drill" discussed previously. The safeties are split into two groups: the tacklers and the ball carriers. At the start of the drill, the safety takes three steps toward the middle of his zone. Then, as the ball carrier passes the tackle, the safety rotates to the flat and, when the ball crosses the line of scrimmage, the safety comes up and makes the tackle. The key coaching point to emphasize in this drill is the outside-in relationship the safety must maintain with the ball carrier. After each tackle, the safety and ball carrier alternate lines. The drill as shown in Diagram 11.11 is done on both sides of the field, usually between the hash marks and the sideline.

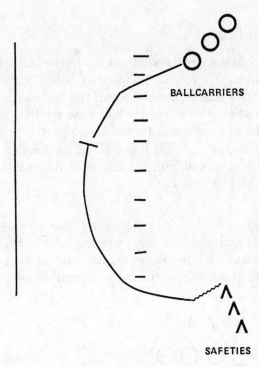

Diagram 11.11

Goal Line Tackling

This is a one on one, head to head tackling drill done within a five yard box on the goal line. The tackler starts with his heels on the goal line and the ball carrier starts with his heels on the five yard line. Dummies are used to complete the five yard box. The drill starts on the movement of the ball carrier, with the object being to stop the touchdown. After each tackle, the players change sides.

There are six drills we do with the safeties which are intended to improve their concentration on the ball and their ability to catch the ball. Some of these drills are the same as the drills we do with our receivers, for we believe catching and concentration are the same whether you are on defense or on offense.

High Point Drill

This drill teaches the safeties to catch the ball at the highest point possible. They must go up for the ball with their arms extended. The safeties cannot expect the ball to come down to them. The safeties form a single line. One at a time they start to back peddle and the coach throws a high pass. The safety must then go up and catch the ball at the highest possible point. The coach emphasizes catching the ball with the hands as well as getting as high as possible.

Tip Drill

In this drill, the first safety tips the ball as high as possible while the second safety catches the ball. Again, the ball must be caught with the hands at the highest possible point. The pass

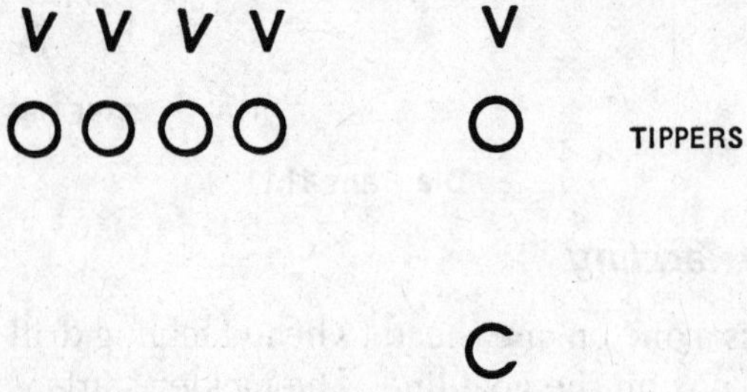

Diagram 11.12

should be thrown just over the head of the first safety. The setup for this drill is shown in Diagram 11.12.

Hot Potato

For this drill, the safeties are split into groups of approximately five players. Each group has a football and forms a circle. The purpose of the drill is to keep the ball moving as quickly as possible throughout the circle for as long as possible, without dropping the ball. The ball is to be thrown to various players, not handed off. We have found the players enjoy this drill and will make it into a competition between the groups.

Turn Around Drill

For this drill, the safeties are broken into groups of approximately five. Each group stands in a line seven yards from a passer. The safeties have their back to the passer. As he releases the ball, the passer calls "ball"; the safeties turn and the one to whom the ball is thrown makes the catch. Again the catch is to be made with the hands. As the drill progresses, the passer throws the ball faster or makes his call later in the release.

Get to the Ball

Two dummies are used for this drill as shown in Diagram 11.13. The passer throws the ball over the dummies and the

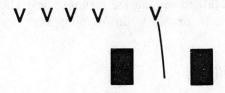

Diagram 11.13

safety must fight his way through the dummies while concentrating on the ball and then make the catch at the highest point possible.

An interesting variation is to use two safeties. Each fights through the dummies to get the ball or to prevent the other safety from catching it.

Distraction Drill

This drill involves having one or two players between the passer and the safety. These players yell, wave their hands and otherwise attempt to distract the safety as he tries to catch the ball.

We feel these drills cover all the areas necessary for our safeties to improve their individual skills. We have enough variety in the drills so that staleness, due to constant repetition of the same drills in every defensive practice, does not become a problem. Our safeties enjoy this segment of practice because they turn this time into a competition among themselves which helps both the individual player and the team.

Group Drills to Stop the Run

In keeping with our concept of simplicity, there are only two drills that are used in the group run period of the defensive practice. Which drill we will do on a given day depends on whether we want to emphasize teaching new alignment variations and stunts or work on reading keys from the basic alignment.

Stunting Drill

The players who are not directly involved in this drill will form an offensive line. Any other players stand behind the offense and watch their position. As shown in Diagram 11.14, the line coach takes a position so he can be sure the linemen maintain their proper alignment throughout the drill. The linebacker coach takes a position to see all of the linebackers. The coach then calls out the stunt to be executed. If this is during the pre-season, we ask "Are there any questions?" before having the center move the ball. On the snap of the ball, all of the defensive players execute the assignment appropriate to the stunt that was called.

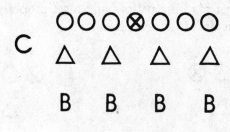

Diagram 11.14

The coaches evaluate their players as to execution of the stunt, things such as: correct stunting technique, maintaining a parallel position with respect to the line of scrimmage, delivering the blow with the proper hand and/or forearm, and getting the proper depth into the backfield. In the pre-season, when this drill is emphasized, the groups are changed quite often so that everyone will learn the stunts being taught during that practice.

Reading Drill

This drill emphasizes reading the appropriate key when not stunting. The inside units work with one of the coaches as shown in Diagram 11.15, and the outside units work with the other coach and set up as shown in Diagram 11.16. During this drill the defenders are always in basic and must react to the blocking pattern of the offense. The exact movement of the defense is dependent on the specific keys developed by the coaching staff. Each week the coaches spend a great deal of time at the scouting meeting working out the keys for the upcoming opponent. To start the drill, the coach, by means of hand signals, gives the offensive players a blocking pattern and a snap count. The defenders must read the pattern and react properly. The initial contact in this drill is always "live."

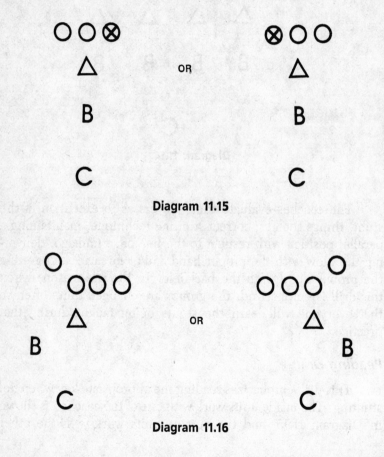

Diagram 11.15

Diagram 11.16

Group Drills to Stop the Pass

Our time in group pass defense is devoted to one drill. Our linebackers and safeties play pass defense as groups of extras run patterns against our various coverages. This "skeleton pass" drill is done quickly, with the emphasis on each defender getting to the proper area. The ball is moved laterally from hash mark to hash mark with either dummies or players representing the offensive tackles. During this part of practice, we spend time on all the coverages we plan to use for the upcoming game.

We also check the positioning of the linebackers and safeties during the team defense segment of practice. The reaction to the ball is always full speed, but we do not tackle in the "skeleton pass" drill.

It is during this segment of practice that the linemen work on their pass rush techniques. This may be done in a one on one situation, or some of the stunts we intend to use in passing situations are worked on.

These are the individual and group drills we use to prepare for our games. As stated in the introduction to this chapter, they are not unique nor are they very complicated. We strive for good execution of a number of basic techniques, then use those techniques in a great number of alignments and stunts to take advantage of our quickness and to challenge the offense.

The material presented in this book has been proven to be very successful for us and I feel sure that it can also be helpful to your program.

12

QUESTIONS AND ANSWERS
REGARDING THE
STUNTING DEFENSE

After completing the preceding chapters, it might be worthwhile to summarize some of the ideas presented and to answer some questions you might have regarding the stunting defense. The following questions are those which coaches in our area, some of whom we play against, ask us regarding our defensive scheme.

HOW OFTEN DO WE ACTUALLY STUNT?

While we do not stunt on every play, we very rarely play the "basic" defense. If alignment variations, short yardage and goal line situations are counted as not being in the basic defense, we might have everyone in basic 2 or 3 plays a game.

HOW OFTEN DO WE STUNT BOTH LINEBACKERS ON THE SAME SIDE?

It is very rare that both linebackers on the same side of the ball (1 and 2 or 3 and 4) will be involved in a stunt. We would have an extremely strong rollout or sprintout tendency to make such a call because there would be no flat coverage against a drop back pass and very little pursuit against a run. If we want to send more than three people on one side of the ball, we use either the 43 blitz or 6-1 with a four deep zone and fire the middle linebacker.

WHEN STUNTING FROM ZONE COVERAGE, HOW ARE THE UNDERNEATH ZONES COVERED?

If only one inside linebacker is stunting, the other compensates and we play three underneath and three deep zones against the drop back pass.

If more than one linebacker is involved in a stunt, we will give up some of the underneath coverage to pressure the ball. The stunt called depends on the pass pattern we expect, so that the vacated zone is one where we do not expect a receiver.

Against a sprintout team, we stunt the outside linebacker to the expected side of the play as the rotation, in the basic pass defense, brings a safety up into the flat.

HOW MUCH MAN COVERAGE IS PLAYED WHEN STUNTING?

As a rule we do not play man coverage from the three deep alignment. The reasons for this are discussed in Chapter 6. This indicates that most of our stunting is done with zone coverage. However, we go to the four deep, man to man coverage in certain situations if we feel we must stop the short passing game or are having trouble covering patterns which flood a particular zone. Also the 4-3 alignment allows for better coverage against teams that try to spread the defense as we will have a free safety to support on the run. Our four deep, man to man can be played from the 4-3, 5-2 or 6-1 alignments.

HOW ARE THE PASS COVERAGES COORDINATED WITH THE STUNTS?

The pass coverages are coordinated by the coaches and become part of the defensive call in the huddle. The linebacker who is making the call must know which personnel (three safeties or four safeties) are in the game. To facilitate this, the fourth safety calls the huddle and is directly in front of the signal caller. When using the three deep, if no pass coverage call is made, we play the rotating zone described in Chapter 4. If the non-rotated zone is to be used, a call is made in the huddle.

When using the four deep, if no pass coverage is called, we play man to man with a free safety as described in Chapter 6. Any other four deep coverage (zone, combination or prevent) must be called in the huddle.

AS THE ALIGNMENTS CHANGE DO THE KEYS ALSO CHANGE?

The keys for the linemen are the same. Whenever they are aligned opposite an offensive player (basic, overshift, 4-3, or goal line) their first job is to defeat the blocker and protect the area not being covered by the linebacker. If, in the 4-4, both members of the unit are playing basic, the lineman usually is responsible for the inside area.

The inside linebacker's key generally is flow through the lineman he is opposite. If the linebacker is opposite a guard (basic or overshift) he reads the guard when he is not stunting. However, if the inside linebacker is opposite the tackle (wide) or center (4-3), he reads the flow of play through the lineman. The linebacker knows he cannot make the play unless he first defeats the blocker.

As discussed in the text, the basic key for the outside linebacker is the end-wing combination. As the offense splits an end out, the outside linebacker, after adjusting, reads the near back (for flow) through the tackle (for run or pass).

WHAT ARE THE LINEBACKER KEYS WHEN PLAYING A TEAM THAT USES A LOT OF MISDIRECTION AS IN THE DELAWARE WING T?

When playing basic against a Delaware Wing T team, the inside linebackers key the guards. We have found that the guards will take us to the point of attack most of the time. We also have had success against the Wing T offense by stunting one of the inside units even though they may not be at the expected point of attack. This has broken up the timing necessary for the offense to be successful and also confused the blocking assignments.

The outside linebackers key the end and near back when not stunting. Whenever flow goes away, the outside linebacker must be aware of the counter, bootleg or reverse.

In any situation where we expect a lot of misdirection from the opponent, we work on reacting to the blocking pattern rather than reading backs when playing basic. The stunts, as usual, are determined by the tendencies of the opposition.

HOW DO WIDEOUTS, AS IN TWINS, AFFECT OUR STUNTING TO THE FORMATION SIDE?

When we use the 4-4 alignment against the wide slot (twins) after our adjustment is made with the outside linebacker, we have three defenders against two blockers (see Diagram 2.15). This still allows for a variety of stunts to the side of the formation such as the gap stunt with the tackle, the X stunt with the inside unit or the loop stunt with the end already on the tackle. Also, if a run is expected, the outside linebacker could cheat toward the ball and execute a crash to the side of the formation.

If there is a very strong tendency to run or sprintout to the wide slot, we could overshift the defense to the slot with the outside linebacker playing pass (a no rotation call) and the defensive end uncovered and pressuring the outside play.

If the offense shows a tendency to run away from the formation, we could then overshift to the tight end. The backside outside linebacker now adjusts to the wide slot. In either situation, any of the overshift stunts, as discussed in Chapter 5, could be used.

ISN'T PLAYING A STUNTING DEFENSE VERY RISKY?

This is the most common question asked regarding the stunting defense. Our experience has been that the answer is a definite NO! Only once in seven years have we given up more than 100 points, and for two consecutive years we were the leading defensive team in our area, allowing 77 points in ten games and then 49 points in eleven games.

A close look at the defensive scheme shows that in every call there is a defender responsible for each area along the line of scrimmage. With an eight man front, someone is responsible for each area along the entire front of the offense. Whenever one member of a unit is stunting, the other player in that unit's first move must be to compensate (move in the opposite direction) for the stunt. It then will become a matter of who is going to better execute his assignment, the blocker or the defender. If the stunting causes any hesitation on the part of the blocker, the advantage will go to the defense.

WITH ALL OF THE POSSIBLE CALLS, DON'T THE PLAYERS EVER GET CONFUSED AND "BLOW" THE CALL?

Our experience has been that our players do *not* get confused. They learn that they must only know what their unit is doing so that while the overall call might get to be a little wordy, they only concentrate on the part of the call that will affect them. We tell *each* unit what they are to do and if their number is not called, they play basic. We have found it to be more of a problem to remember our offensive assignments, as the calls don't tell each player what to do.

SINCE THERE IS SO MUCH MOVEMENT, AREN'T THERE MANY TECHNIQUES THAT MUST BE TAUGHT?

NO! One of the great advantages of this defense is that the number of techniques for each group is very limited. For example, the initial movement for a lineman in the gap, slant, cross and twist stunts is exactly the same. The player takes an open step in the direction of the call, and depending on the specific stunt, moves over one man, two men or through the gap. The initial movement of the linebackers, whether scraping or firing, is also the same. Simplicity is a very important part of this defensive program.

WHAT TYPE OF ATHLETE IS USED TO PLAY THE LINEBACKER POSITIONS?

The success of the stunting defense depends on how well our linebackers can execute the stunts and be sure tacklers. Quickness, discipline and aggressiveness are the qualities we look for in all our defensive players. The linebackers normally are in the 150-170 pound range as it should be remembered that the front four are usually under 200 pounds each. From time to time we have had some success in moving a safety who might be too slow to play deep pass coverage, if he has some size, up to play linebacker.

WHAT ARE THE PHYSICAL DIFFERENCES BETWEEN THE INSIDE UNITS AND THE OUTSIDE UNITS?

The primary difference is the agility of the front four people. As discussed in the text, after the four best defensive linemen have been determined, we place the more agile of them at the end positions and the other two become the tackles. We also try to balance the defensive front so that the two best defensive players are not playing next to each other. Over the years we have had equal success with the best linemen playing 1 and 3 positions as compared to having the best linemen playing the 2 and 4 positions. All the other linemen must be able to play anywhere along the defensive front. One year, due to injuries, we moved a starting tackle over to defensive end because he was more agile than the substitute end, and we allowed only two touchdowns and one field goal in four games after the switch.

The ability to play pass coverage and discipline in forcing the outside run are the prime considerations in determining which of the starting linebackers will play on the outside. Once this has been decided, the actual placement is done in a way that the better of the linebackers is paired with the weaker of the linemen. Our goal is to present as balanced a front as possible (quick linebacker with slower lineman, etc.). One exception is left handed personnel. If possible, we place our left handed linemen on the left side of the defense (inside responsibility) and left handed linebackers on the right side of the defense (outside responsibility).

DOES MOTION CHANGE ANY STUNTS?

Generally, motion will not change a stunt call. We are going to stunt at the expected point of attack and whether motion is used usually will not alter that tendency.

However, extended motion might force us to call off any outside stunts, such as the crash, so that the outside linebacker can help with the quick pass to the motion man or be in a better position to defend the crack back block. This decision is made at the weekly scouting meeting and worked on during the week in practice.

HOW DOES MOTION CHANGE THE PERIMETER DEFENSE?

When we are playing zone coverage, short motion (between the ends) does not change the perimeter defense. Extended motion causes the safeties to adjust their alignment. The outside safety moves with the man in motion to maintain the position he would take on a flanker which is discussed in Chapter 2.

If we are in basic, three deep coverage, the middle safety aligns deeper as the man in motion gets closer to the sideline. Also, if the ball is on a hash mark, the middle safety moves toward the middle of the field. These adjustments are made so that the middle safety will be able to cover the man in motion in the deep outside one third of the field should he have to rotate.

When playing man to man, the defender assigned to the receiver moves along as he goes in motion. The free safety adjusts to help on any overload to the wide side if the ball is on a hash mark.

Whenever a man in motion goes past the tight end, the outside linebacker loosens with him until there is no threat of a crack back. When the motion becomes extended, the outside linebacker moves back to his normal alignment. The linebacker, in basic, has contain and must not allow the man in motion to get outside leverage on him. On the snap, the linebacker will get to a position where the man in motion cannot legally block him. The linebacker must be on the opposition's side of the line of scrimmage so that the man in motion cannot get his head in front for a legal crack back block. If the ball goes away from the motion, the linebacker contains and then drops back in his rotation on a pass or pursue on a run.

ARE FIELD TENDENCIES USED OR DO WE RELY ONLY ON DOWN AND DISTANCE TENDENCIES?

Normally we rely more heavily on down and distance or formation tendencies than on field position. However, there are some exceptions. A turnover by our offense, as discussed in Chapter 10, could cause us to try to be more aggressive in forcing a mistake. A strong tendency to throw or not throw from a certain area of the field would have an effect on our call. Also field position and the number of time outs would strongly influence the calls made at the end of the half or the end of the game.

WHAT IS DONE TO AVOID BEING TRAPPED WHEN STUNTING?

The aiming point on all of the stunts is one yard penetration into the backfield.

If no blocker is coming at the defender, the defender closes to the inside until he can locate the ball. The move to the inside is made so that the defender does not turn his body and will take on the trap block with the inside arm while remaining parallel to the line of scrimmage. The defender is taught to "push" the blocker back into the hole and create a pile at the point of attack.

DO WE STUNT ONLY TO COMPENSATE FOR WEAKER PERSONNEL?

One of the primary reasons we changed to the stunting defense was the difficulty we had with our personnel being able to control a blocker and then make the defensive play for a minimal gain. We felt that year in and year out we would not get enough players who would be able to read successfully.

Since the introduction of the stunting defense, we have had a few 220-230 pound defensive linemen who were capable of controlling the offensive blockers. However, we found the big, slow players were not an advantage. It is our feeling that, regardless of size, aggressiveness and quickness are the important attributes to being successful. A quick, aggressive smaller player will help your program more than a big, slow player. The big, quick, aggressive player is every coach's dream.

Football is an aggressive game, and if any of us are fortunate enough to have those big, quick, aggressive players let them be aggressive on defense as well as on offense. Why should the player be aggressive and "fire out" on offense and have to read and react on defense? If you have smaller players, then your only chance for success is to sell them on quickness and aggressiveness. Again, by stunting and attacking the offense you can develop that aggressive attitude that is essential to success.

Appendix

TIME SCHEDULE FOR TEACHING
THE STUNTING DEFENSE

As indicated in Chapter 10, we devote approximately one half of our practice time to defense. In New Jersey, we must practice for at least seven days before our first scrimmage, which, depending on how early school opens, will give us between four and six defensive practice sessions before the first scrimmage. This is because our double session practices before school opens consist of one offensive practice and one defensive practice. Within these limits, we have developed a five day practice schedule for the teaching of our total defensive program.

In those years in which there are only four defensive practices before the first scrimmage, we adhere to this schedule and introduce the special situation defenses after the first scrimmage. We then use the remaining scrimmages as a review by using as many different combinations as possible. We are more concerned with our performance and knowledge of the defense than we are with "winning" a scrimmage. The chart shows the breakdown of this teaching progression.

Note that the linebackers are given a handout with all the formations we expect to see during the upcoming season. They must learn to recognize each formation and make the proper adjustments as presented in Chapter 2 of the text.

PRE-SEASON PRACTICES

	LINEMEN	LINEBACKERS	SAFETIES
DAY 1	1. Basic alignment	1. Basic alignment	1. Basic 3 deep alignment
	2. Stance	2. Form tackle	2. Non-rotating 3 deep coverage
	3. Neutralize blocker	3. Stack, wide, tight variations	
	4. Stack variation	4. Fire, X, loop stunts	
	5. Gap, slant, X, loop stunts	5. Non-rotating pass coverage	
DAY 2	1. Review day 1	1. Review day 1	1. Review day 1
	2. Crash, cross, jam stunts	2. Start shed, scrape techniques	2. Work on 3 deep rotation
	3. Pass rush drills	3. Crash, jam stunts	3. Teach formation adjustments
		4. Rotating zone pass coverage	

DAY 3	1. Review basic techniques 2. Overshift alignment and variations (nose, eagle, stack, under)	1. Review basic techniques 2. Overshift alignment and variations (nose, eagle, stack, under)	1. Review 3 deep coverages 2. Start work on man to man coverage
DAY 4	1. Review overshift alignment and variations 2. Overshift stunts inside X, outside X, front and back	1. Work with linemen on overshift alignment, variations and stunts	1. Review 3 deep zone and man to man coverages 2. Introduce 4 deep zone
DAY 5	1. Review defense to date 2. Special situation defenses—43 with stunts and goal line	1. Review defense to date 2. Special situation defenses—43 with stunts and goal line	1. Review 3 deep zone 2. Work on 4 deep zone 3. Teach combination coverage

INDEX